EXPERIENCING CHRIST
WITHIN

Passionately Embracing God's Provisions
for Supernatural Living

EXPERIENCING CHRIST
WITHIN

A COMPANION WORKBOOK FOR REVOLUTION WITHIN

DWIGHT EDWARDS

WATERBROOK
PRESS

EXPERIENCING CHRIST WITHIN
PUBLISHED BY WATERBROOK PRESS
12265 Oracle Boulevard, Suite 200
Colorado Springs, Colorado 80921
A division of Random House, Inc.

Quotations from *Revolution Within:* © 2001 by Dwight Edwards

ISBN 1-57856-540-5

Published in association with Yates & Yates, LLP, Literary Agent, Orange, California.

Library of Congress Cataloging-in-Publication Data
Edwards, Dwight, 1954-
    Experiencing Christ within : passionately embracing God's provisions for supernatural living / Dwight Edwards.—1st ed.
        p. cm.
    ISBN 1-57856-540-5
        1. Christian life. I. Title.

BV4501.3 .E38 2001
248.4—dc21

2001046635

Printed in the United States of America
2006

10 9 8 7 6

Contents

THE PRACTICAL OUTWORKING OF SUPERNATURAL LIVING

Let Your Heart Dream

Is it really possible that before Christ returns, His Spirit may once again move in revival power? Might there be another Great Awakening that stirs the church to first tremble before God and then pant after Him?

It would take deep brokenness, something we've trivialized into merely facing the wounds from our past. And it would require repentance, which to many moderns means little more than admitting we need help and going for counseling.

If we faced how shallow and powerless our lives have become, how self-absorbed and ruled by a spirit of entitlement we actually are, perhaps we would be transformed from a community of the comfortable (or at least trying to be) into the community of the broken. And if that happened, maybe the Spirit would continue His work by turning us into a community of hope, men and women praying fervently for another "time of refreshing" from the Lord.

Our weighty God is right now sitting lightly on His church. To the watching world, He must seem more a shiny veneer decorating our lives than our sure foundation. Good things, of course, are happening—the Spirit is faithfully building Christ's church—but as one pastor recently put it to me: "Something's missing. I see obvious blessing, and I know it's God's hand. But sometimes I envision what the Spirit must long to do in God's people, and I wonder if anything real is happening at all. I know it is, but there could be so much more."

I wonder if any of us look at Christ and, in the middle of terrible trial, say He is enough and mean it? Or watch cherished dreams shatter and with renewed vigor pursue the greater dream of knowing Him better, and do so with gratitude for the privilege? Do any of us know what it is to suffer betrayal and rejection and count it all joy, not only that we're deemed worthy to suffer for the name but also that now we have a unique opportunity to reveal what Christ is like to our abusers? Do we value knowing God and glorifying Him—no matter what's happening in our lives—ever depending on God and letting Him make our lives more fulfilling?

I worry that we've twisted the message of the Cross into a promise that God will provide us enough creature comforts on earth, whether material or spiritual, to keep the journey to heaven reasonably pleasant till we get there. We think it's His job to see to it that we feel pretty good here till we feel forever good there. Modern Christianity, in dramatic reversal of its biblical form, is now all about us.

God hasn't checked with me on this (or on anything else), but I sense that He may be setting the stage for another *reformation* that, coupled with true *revival,* could spark a *revolution* in the church.

The first reformation recovered with liberating clarity the truth of *how* we're made right with God, how we receive God's life and the guarantee of enjoying it forever. I suggest that the reformation needed in the church today would focus on *why* God gives us life, on the real reason that Jesus died. "It is not for your sake…that I am going to do these things," God said, "but for the sake of my holy name" (Ezekiel 36:22, NIV).

The Spirit would cut through our narcissistic nuttiness to make clear that God saved us in order for Him to receive glory, not to help us feel good about ourselves and lead exciting lives. We would see that Christ's blood was shed so that, as forgiven disciples, we might trust God when life falls apart rather than expecting Him to keep it together. Light would dispel the fog that prevents us from seeing anything beyond our own longings, and we would realize that life—our relationships, our health, our bank accounts, our time—is not all about us. It's all about God.

He's the star of the show. We would see that we're bit players, and we'd be thrilled that we're part of the drama. No suffering would be viewed as unfair for us to endure if it helped keep the spotlight on Christ. That would be a turnabout, a reformation in our understanding of what God is up to in the gospel.

Revival would follow. The Spirit would convince us that under the terms of God's new arrangement with people—the New Covenant brought in at Pentecost that replaced the old one begun at Sinai—God has done more than we think. We've not only been forgiven so completely that the Father now sings over us with delight at every moment from conversion on, but He has also changed us, deeply, profoundly, permanently. Under the new arrangement we're not merely ordered to glorify God, now we *want* to. And we're equipped to do it. It becomes actually possible, we see it as our highest privilege and joy, to revolve our lives around God.

We discover an appetite within us that prefers the pleasures of holiness to the pleasures of sin. With Augustine, we actually experience the joy of knowing God's love as greater than the very real fun of sexual release—and so we overcome our addictions and express our sexuality within moral boundaries. We experience the pleasure of His company and the privilege of being in His service as far surpassing all lesser pleasures and privileges. And so we mature; we become more like Christ. We lead changed (though still imperfect) lives that reveal a new power in our makeup that puzzles people who watch.

We were saved to glorify God. Realizing that one truth is the heart of the reformation that the modern church must experience. And our salvation provides us with all the resources we need to pull it off. Having that realization and learning how to draw on those resources will begin the revival. Our lives can actually be all about God and not about us. That's the coming revolution.

Think about it. Let your heart dream. From narcissists to worshipers. From people trying hard to make our lives more pleasing to us, to people who make it our priority to please God. Men would turn off their cable pornography. Lonely women would no longer date still-married men. People with limited means would be glad when their friends got rich. Children would spend time with their aging parents and count it a privilege to do so. We'd stop being so damnably selfish and actually be more concerned for others than for ourselves, even when the price was high. The church would shift from a fractious society of ego-driven competitors whose souls never meet to a gathering of broken, grateful saints ruled by the passion of grace. We'd become a *community*.

If the Spirit reforms our understanding of why God bothered to save us in the first place, if He revives our passion to live sacrificially for Him without focusing on our own immediate sense of well-being, a revolution will be set in motion. The church will be on its way again to being the church, never perfectly of course, but perhaps as substantially as in the days of Acts.

This workbook, written by my close friend and colleague Dwight Edwards, could help trigger that revolution. With the passion of a man on a mission from God and with the power of a writer who listens to the Spirit as his fingers move across the keyboard, Dwight lays the foundation for both reformation and revival, the reformation and revival the modern church desperately needs.

I remember when he called me from his home in Texas to say, "Larry, something just hit me. God introduced the New Covenant to pull His name out of the mud. I've read it before in Ezekiel—it's plain as day—but now I see it. The gospel is all about God's glory; it's not about my fulfillment. But living for His glory guarantees my fulfillment!" He was nearly shouting.

Another call, a few months later: "I'm realizing that the gospel actually changes who we are, not just our legal position before God. The pressure's off! Now I can glorify God by releasing who I really am. Larry, we've missed the thrill of New Covenant living. It's far better than most of us have ever imagined. I thought my job as a pastor was to persuade people to do what they really didn't want to do and to act like people they really weren't. But my calling is to tell them what God has done, stir up their holy appetites, provide some basic direction, and turn 'em loose."

Experiencing Christ Within is all about theology. But you'll think it's an exciting story. Of course that's what theology is. It's the exciting story of God, who He is and what He's doing, especially with us.

Open your heart to the Spirit as you slowly work through these pages. This workbook may jump-start the revolution you've longed for in yourself, in your small group, and in your church. As never before, you may experience supernatural living, a life that's all about God and a freedom to live out who you really are, a lover of God. The revolution within has already happened. This workbook will make that clear. After digesting its message, you'll want to make the revolution visible.

—DR. LARRY CRABB

Questions You May Have About This Workbook

What will this workbook do for me?

Experiencing Christ Within—a companion to the book *Revolution Within*—is a thorough exploration, with interwoven Bible study questions, of New Covenant truths that are the foundation for all effective personal change in the Christian life. It is a guide to appropriating their power to ignite vital intimacy with God, to give us genuine community with one another, and to launch us with hope into kingdom warfare.

The *Experiencing Christ Within* workbook will help you—in a practical and spiritually reflective way—to appreciate and to appropriate four lavish supernatural resources that God has placed within every believer: a new purity, a new disposition, a new identity, and a new power. You will discover profoundly that in fulfillment of God's New Covenant promises to each of us, these revolutionary provisions are residing permanently within your soul right now, ready for release every day of your life on earth.

Is this workbook enough, or do I also need the book *Revolution Within*?

Experiencing Christ Within includes many of the major points covered in *Revolution Within,* plus others. The added interactive elements of Bible study and life-response questions will help you biblically test and explore these principles from *Revolution Within* for yourself and then apply the biblical teachings to your life under the Holy Spirit's counsel. So having a copy of *Revolution Within* as you go through this workbook would be helpful but is not essential.

(The number of each weekly lesson in *Experiencing Christ Within* is the same as the corresponding chapter number in *Revolution Within;* Week Thirteen—the final lesson in *Experiencing Christ Within*—parallels chapters 13–16 in *Revolution Within.*)

The lessons look long. Do I need to work through all of each one?

This thirteen-lesson workbook is designed to promote your thorough exploration of each week's material, but you may find it best to focus your time and discussion on some sections and questions more than others. However, we make no apology for the length of the lessons, as we strongly believe this content (especially the scriptures you'll explore) can bring radical life change.

Also, you may decide to follow a slower pace than one lesson per week. This could be true whether you're going through *Experiencing Christ Within* individually or in a group. In a group that meets weekly, for example, you may decide to spend two weeks of discussion time on each lesson. (You may especially want to do this for the final lesson, which is longer than the others.) In your first meeting, decide together on what you believe to be the best pacing and schedule.

If you're going through *Experiencing Christ Within* on your own, you may simply want to try completing two or three questions each day.

Above all, keep in mind that the purpose of *Experiencing Christ Within* is to help guide you in specific life-application of the New Covenant truths taught in *Revolution Within.* The wide assortment of questions included in each weekly lesson is meant to help you approach this practical application from different angles, and with expansive reflection and self-examination.

Allowing adequate time to prayerfully reflect on each question will be much more valuable for you than rushing through *Experiencing Christ Within.*

Ready for Release

Do you hunger for more in your Christian experience than you're tasting right now? Are you weary of trying again and again to fix old patterns that stubbornly refuse to budge? Is there a dullness and dryness to your spirituality that you can't seem to shake?

You may be much closer than you ever imagined to significant breakthroughs—because of a revolution that happened within you when you trusted Christ, a revolution whose full power is awaiting release.

SOMETHING FOR THE NOW

I've never been particularly adept with mechanical things. This once again became apparent a few years ago when we purchased a new lawn mower for our home. My wife and son picked it out, which was fine with me; all I wanted to know was where to put the gas and how to start it.

After about six months with this new mower, I noticed an interesting thing. It took my son about half as long to mow our lawn as it did me, and he was far less sweaty afterwards. I attributed this to the benefit of youth.

One day when I was mowing, he approached me and said he wanted to show me something about what I was doing. I was skeptical; after all, I'd been mowing long before he was born. But I decided to humor him and let him have his say.

"See that lever?" He pointed to the left side of the mower. "Now pull it down."

3

When I did, the engine connected somehow with the front wheels, and they began turning on their own. It was great! Now I understood my son's secret—he was utilizing a resource I never even knew was available.

In a similar way, I believe many, many believers launch out to accomplish what they know God has told them to do—but in their own strength, relying only on their own resources. They grit their teeth and press forward, yet inwardly their souls are wilting under the unbearable weight of God's commands. God's promise of rest for their souls (Matthew 11:28-30) seems more a mockery than a possibility.

The good news of the gospel is more than forgiveness of sins and a guarantee of heaven in the future. *God has given us something for the now,* a present resource of monumental proportions for accomplishing radical, abandoned discipleship. But if we don't really understand these resources, we'll find it difficult to appropriate them in any significant way.

This is why I'm so excited about this study. I'm gripped to the core of my being by two central convictions: (1) Many believers really don't know in any substantial way *who they are in Christ* and *what He has provided for them* in terms of present godly living. (2) There's a present hope for godly living provided through Christ alone that brings a quality and significance of life beyond what most of us ever thought possible. It's called the New Covenant. And it makes a real difference, in real people, to the glory of God alone.

Why, then, are more Christians not appropriating these great realities made possible through God alone? One of the main reasons, I believe, is that they are tragically unaware of the radical nature of their new birth.

A CAR WASH—AND THE GUN AT MY HEAD

Something like a car wash is how many Christians view their conversion: You go in a filthy clunker; you come out with your sins washed away—a cleansed clunker.

Such cleansing indeed happened when we became Christians, but *so much more* transpired as well! It's as if, right there between the power wash and power rinse cycles, a brand-new engine was dropped into the car, plus entirely new wiring. Of course the old engine is temporarily left in, and we can choose (foolishly) to operate by it and to live like the clunker we were. But *we don't have to*—because of a divine revolution within.

It's a revolution we learn more about in what I believe are some of the most powerful yet badly neglected realities in all the Word of God.

One day about fifteen years ago I was chatting with a friend and gifted counselor, and he made this observation: "Dwight, you live with the word *should* pointed to your head like a gun." I honestly didn't know at the time if this was a compliment or a rebuke. After all, the key to the Christian life, as best I understood it, was commitment and obedience—carrying out all the "should's" that Scripture is filled with.

Another word that described my spiritual life in those days was *pressured.* I was seeking to live up to the vast array of God's standards that seemed to press down on me relentlessly. Most of the standards I held for myself were totally legitimate and based on the Word of God. But what I'd never heard before in any substantive fashion was the staggering news that *God* has provided us with the "want's" for His "should's."

God used that conversation with my friend, plus a tape series on freedom by Larry Crabb, to launch me on my own pilgrimage into what the Bible calls the New Covenant. Along the way I've continued to discover a hope for present Christian living that I never knew existed. Perplexing verses such as "His commandments are not burdensome" (1 John 5:3) have begun to make sense. I discovered that through the New Covenant the burden is lifted because of the new disposition and new power God has given for carrying out His standards.

I have far, far to go in fully appropriating this reality; on this earth I always will. But the little ground God has allowed me to cover has deeply convinced me that there's a genuine rest of soul, a joyfulness of spirit, and an unpressured spirituality that come only through the wondrous provisions of the New Covenant.

What exactly is the New Covenant? And what real difference can it make for our lives? The exciting answers to those two questions are what this workbook is all about.

SO WHAT'S NEW?

If you're thinking, *So what's the big deal about the New Covenant?* I can identify. I spent many years as a believer and even as a pastor thinking I knew pretty well what the New Covenant was all about: Jesus shedding His blood for our sins and justifying us by His righteousness. What I hadn't realized was how much *more* the New Covenant provided.

Four core convictions have arisen in my heart over the years as I have studied and pursued this great theme of Scripture. These convictions will be fleshed out in greater detail throughout the workbook, but I want to introduce them to you at the outset:

1. The *promises* found in the New Covenant are *the kindling with which the fire of vital intimacy with God is ignited.*

2. The *resources* provided by the New Covenant are *the lifeblood of genuine community.*

3. The *hope* stimulated by the New Covenant is *the launching pad for kingdom warfare.*

4. And the *realities* contained in the New Covenant are *the foundation for all personal change.*

> "The whole dispensation of the Spirit, the whole economy of grace in Christ Jesus, the whole of our spiritual life, the whole of the health and strength of the church, has been laid down and provided for and secured in the New Covenant."
>
> —Andrew Murray

I've seen time and again how much difference these truths make in everyday life. In fact, they deal more with how we *live* than how we're saved; they aren't just theological jargon but life-changing realities.

Where Is the Gospel's Power?

Late one night I received a visit from Greg, a twenty-five-year-old single who had been growing in his faith for several years. That day, however, he'd given in to homosexual urges that seemed to overwhelm him.

I'll never forget the look of anguish and desperation etched upon his face that night as he described the intensity of the battle raging within. There was no question in his mind that what he'd done was wrong, that he hated that part of himself, that he would dearly love to be free from these wayward longings. But they were so unbearably strong that he honestly wondered if he had any hope of substantial change.

I was deeply perplexed over what to tell Greg. He was a committed believer sincerely pursuing Christ. He was already doing most of the prescribed disciplines for godliness—quiet time, Scripture memorization, prayer, Bible study, fellowship, sharing his faith, involvement in ministry. Yet, in his greatest hour of need, they all seemed impotent to restrain his sin. Why didn't the gospel have more power in the life of one who truly wanted to change? What would it take to fix Greg in this area?

This same scenario is repeated daily in thousands of forms—the mother whose quick temper erupts all too frequently toward her children, the husband who can't shake free from the chains of pornography, the pastor who cannot overcome his bitterness toward a board member, the teenager who violates his conscience for the approval of his peers. All of us have areas in our lives where we recognize an undeniable chasm between knowing what we should do and actually doing it. The answer to fixing these faults continues to elude us.

Not Fixing, But Releasing

True breakthroughs will never come, however, if we keep working to get ourselves "fixed." They will come only as we embark on a completely new journey.

That journey is what this workbook is all about. It's an expedition focused not on *fixing* but on *releasing*.

Let me tell you more about Greg, who came to me in such desperation. Today he's happily married, a wonderful father, walking closely with God, and having significant ministry in his job and church. Does he ever face temptation toward homosexuality? Yes, but not nearly as much. Greg is a wonderful example of what Francis Schaeffer called "substantial healing." His transformation isn't total (no one's is, this side of eternity), but it is very, very substantial. There were a number of things God used in his life to help bring about this healing, including good counseling, loving friends, and a helpful church. But Greg would tell you that far and away the most important was this: *the discovery, appropriation, and release of the divine resources provided through the New Covenant.*

Knowing and releasing these resources has strengthened and sustained me in my own spiritual pilgrimage time and again. Certainly I continue to battle daily with my flesh. There are times when I feel so overwhelmed by guilt, lust, fear, or anger that I wonder if I'll ever get past my perverse sin nature. But through the New Covenant I've discovered the good news of *another reality*—that beneath all my sin, all the dysfunction of my past, all my insecurities, all my rebellion, there resides a radical new nature, implanted and sustained by God alone. Sometimes that new

> "To the great loss of the church, the rich vein of truth contained in the scriptural teaching concerning the old and new covenants is practically unexplored and unexamined today."
>
> —J. Oswald Sanders

nature seems elusive, especially when it's covered over by other competing passions. But while it doesn't seem real, that doesn't mean it isn't real. Because of the New Covenant, I know God has infused me with a new nature of His own making that can never be diminished or removed.

That's why the great issue in Christian living is not how to get ourselves fixed but *how to get our new nature released.*

Come, my friend, and let's explore how to do just that. Let's learn more about this new reality that God has called us to…that He's also deeply inclined our hearts toward…and that He's also fully empowered us to carry out.

A Brand-New Arrangement

Discipleship is built entirely on the supernatural grace of God.

OSWALD CHAMBERS

1. (a) As you begin, how would you express your personal goals or expectations for the time you'll spend working through *Experiencing Christ Within?* Record your thoughts here: *I desire to know + experience Jesus Christ as I was created to when He gifted me w/salvation. I want His Spirit to be evident in me + work/live through me daily. I want to have truly a new life and experience it to the fullest, trusting Him. + not my flesh in every situation*

(b) Take a moment to pray and ask God to open your eyes and heart to whatever adjustments He wants to make in your beliefs and daily practices.

FROM GOD: SOMETHING NEW AND DIFFERENT

A profoundly interesting word—*covenant*—is used often in Scripture for God's dealings or arrangements with humanity, such as certain agreements He made with Noah, Abraham, and David. One especially major covenant he made was with Moses and the nation of Israel after they came out of Egypt. This so-called Old Covenant is also known throughout Scripture as "the law."

But later we encounter what God calls "a new covenant," promised through the Old Testament prophets and taught more fully in our New Testament. From the first mention of it, God states that it will be wholly unlike the law.

In this lesson we'll explore the fundamental differences between the Old Covenant and the New. We'll look also at God's purpose for the Law and at the radical difference the New Covenant makes in our approach to spirituality.

2. With an open and eager mind, read the Lord's words to the prophet Jeremiah in Jeremiah 31:31-34. (We'll be coming back often to this foundational New Covenant passage.) In verses 31-32, God emphasizes that the New Covenant will *not* be like (or "not according to") the older covenant He made with His people after bringing them out of Egypt. In verse 32, what does God point out about their response to the older covenant?

   They broke the older covenant, even though He loved them as a husband loves his wife. :)

3. Continue your careful study of this important passage in Jeremiah 31 by answering these questions:

   (a) What does the Lord promise to do for His people in verse 33?

   He'll put His laws in their minds & write them on their hearts. He'll be their God & they'll be their people. 12

(b) What further promise from God do you see at the end of verse 34?

who They won't need to teach their people or neighbors His because everyone will already know Him.

(c) What effects of the New Covenant are foretold in verse 34?

He will forgive our wickedness & will never again remember our sins.

4. Now turn to [Hebrews 8, and notice (beginning in verse 8) that Jeremiah 31:31-34 is quoted in full—here in the heart of a New Testament book that teaches the exalted supremacy and ministry of Christ. That's how important these New Covenant promises are!

(a) In Hebrews 8:6 (just before the Jeremiah passage is quoted), how is the New Covenant described?

As a better covenant w/ God, based on better promises.

(b) In Hebrews 8:13 (immediately after the Jeremiah quotation), how is the Old Covenant described? And what do you think this means?

As obsolete. It's now out of date and ready to be put aside. NO LONGER BENOFICIAL OR USOFUL.

5. Another message from God with New Covenant content is found in (Ezekiel 36:25-27.) What promises from God for His people do you see here? (You'll find a central promise in each of these three verses; each promise is expressed in more than one way.)

He'll cleanse us w/ clean water & our filth will be washed away. He's to give us a new heart w/ new desires & He'll put a new Spirit in us. Take out our stony heart & give us a new obedient heart. His Spirit will live in us.

THE NEW COVENANT:
FOR US OR FOR ISRAEL?

One of the critical issues about such Old Testament passages as Jeremiah 31:31-34 is how this New Covenant applies to the church today. Clearly the promises of the New Covenant were originally addressed to the nation of Israel (to "the house of Israel" and "the house of Judah," as Jeremiah 31:31 says). How then can the church legitimately claim these promises for herself? The issue is complex, and in this brief setting I'll highlight only two significant points in my understanding of it.

(1) The promises of the New Covenant will find their ultimate and complete fulfillment with the nation of Israel in what is often referred to as the "millennial kingdom." However, the church has entered *now* into a strong foretaste of the New Covenant's spiritual blessings. Like the kingdom of God, the New Covenant is "now, but not yet."

(2) New Testament authors as well as Jesus Himself provide us more than sufficient warrant for applying to ourselves the spiritual blessings of the New Covenant. In Luke 22:20 we find Christ's unmistakable assertion that the New Covenant was about to be inaugurated through His death: "This cup is the new covenant in My blood, which is shed for you."

Other references in the New Testament that indicate or imply our present participation in the New Covenant include Romans 2:28-29; 2 Corinthians 3:1-18 and 6:16; Galatians 3:13-14; 5:6; and 6:15; Philippians 3:3; Colossians 2:11-12; Hebrews 7:18-22; 8:6-13; 9:15; 10:9-25; 12:24; and many others.

THE LAW—GOOD OR BAD?

6. So was the *Old* Covenant essentially bad? Was the law itself to blame for the failure by God's people to obey Him? Is the law even to blame for *our* failure to obey God? How would you answer these questions from what you see in Romans 3:31 and 7:12 and Hebrews 8:7-8?

We can't forget about the law. In fact, only when we have faith do we truly fulfill the law. However, God did find fault w/ the old covenant & that's why He established a new covenant.

SO HARD TO LET GO

The two sharpest distinctives of this liberating New Covenant are its *radical difference* from the law, and its *radical superiority* to it.

And why should that concern us?

YOU SHALL VS. I WILL

In the Old Covenant, God's people were instructed with the repeated words, "You shall..." and "You shall not..."

But in the New Covenant, the watchword is no longer "You shall," but God's "I will": "*I will* put My law in their minds...and *I will* be their God.... *I will* forgive their iniquity"; "*I will* cleanse you.... *I will* give you a new heart.... *I will* put My Spirit within you and cause you to walk in My statutes" (Jeremiah 31:33-34; Ezekiel 36:25-27).

Nothing is more fundamental to understanding and appreciating the difference between the two covenants than these two phrases.

Because it's harder than most of us think to fully let go of a law-based approach to spirituality. Our flesh naturally gravitates toward legalistic approaches to holiness that encourage at least some reliance on self. A blend of God's helping us and our helping God is both reasonable and enticing to our fallen nature. It enables us to partially share credit with God for any spiritual success. Most of all, it keeps our pride at least somewhat intact.

7. Paul used strong words in talking to the Galatians about this issue of a law-based approach to Christianity. For example, look at his statements to them in Galatians 3:1-3 and 4:8-9. What are the negatives he pointed out for law-based spirituality? *They forgot that they didn't receive the Holy Spirit by keeping the law. The Holy Spirit came only after they believed in Christ.*

MAKE A CLEAN BREAK

But what's really so wrong about mixing a little Old Covenant into our lives? Won't it cause people to live more fully for God?

The New Testament warns us, however, to give up law-based spirituality or suffer significant spiritual consequences. True spirituality requires an absolutely clean

---

THE GLORY OF GOD'S LAW

"The law of the LORD is *perfect...*" (Psalm 19:7). The psalmists rightly understood this perfection and rejoiced in it: "Oh, how I love Your law! It is my meditation all the day" (Psalm 119:97).

The same message comes through in the words of Isaiah the prophet: "It pleased the LORD for the sake of his righteousness to make his law great and glorious" (Isaiah 42:21, NIV).

---

break from the old way of doing things, replacing it with a radically new approach to God-honoring living.

Jesus had this in mind when He said,

> No one sews a piece of unshrunk cloth on an old garment; or else the
> new piece pulls away from the old, and the tear is made worse. And
> no one puts new wine into old wineskins; or else the new wine bursts
> the wineskins, the wine is spilled, and the wineskins are ruined. But
> new wine must be put into new wineskins. (Mark 2:21-22)

Here He makes two highly significant points concerning His relationship with the old system, the law.

First, *Jesus did not come to patch up the Old Covenant.* He brought in a brand new garment, not a stitch job on an old one.

Second, *Jesus did not come to fit into the old system, but to cleanly replace it.* Like new wine, He is too powerful and vibrant to be confined by the old.

In both cases the message is this: If you mingle these two realities—Old and New Covenants—you end up ruining the whole lot. It's like mixing diesel with regular gas in your car; at best, it will only sputter. The New Covenant doesn't try to salvage what it can from the old but cleanly replaces it with the new.

Is there some sputtering because of a wrong mix in your spiritual engine? Or does your life manifest the supernatural outflow of the indwelling life of Christ, which is the essence of the New Covenant? Let me say it again: *The normal Christian life is nothing more or less than the outflowing of the indwelling Christ.*

"No Throwing Rocks"

This is why the key to the Christian life is *not* obedience to God's standards.

That statement may sound like out-and-out heresy to you, so let me hasten to say that obedience to God's standards is a hugely important part of Christian living. One cannot honestly read the New Testament without coming to this conclusion. But in true spirituality, obedience to God's standards is the by-product and inevitable result of something that's centrally more important.

One of the main reasons the obedience demanded by the law could not produce spirituality in God's people is the effect law has on our flesh. Years ago I was camping beside a river. I'd been there only a few minutes when I saw a sign: "No Throwing Rocks into the River." Guess what? Suddenly I was overcome with a tremendous urge to throw at least one rock into the river. It never even occurred to me to throw a rock until I read that sign, but the law of the campsite aroused the rebellion in my flesh. (I'll leave you guessing as to whether I actually threw it.)

THE TRAGEDY OF THE OLD COVENANT

The law we find presented in the opening books of the Old Testament is saturated with the concept of "covenant."

The core of what we term the Old Covenant is contained in the Ten Commandments, which are called "the words of the covenant" (Exodus 34:28), while the full law given by God at Mount Sinai is called "the Book of the Covenant" (Exodus 24:7).

The tablets of stone on which the Ten Commandments were written were known as the "tablets of the covenant" (Deuteronomy 9:9), and the chest inside the tabernacle (and later in the temple) where these tablets were kept was called the "ark of the covenant" (Hebrews 9:2-4).

As God was preparing to give the Ten Commandments to Moses, He told His people, "Now therefore, if you will indeed obey My voice and *keep My covenant*, then you shall be a special treasure to Me above all people" (Exodus 19:5). He later made clear that to

When God's standards press down upon us, our flesh inevitably rises up in rebellion. Paul noted that our "sinful passions...were aroused by the law" (Romans 7:5). Ever since the Fall, our flesh has been hostile to God's rule in our lives. *The law cannot change this hostility, but only further aggravates it.*

That's a big part of why God had to do something radically new in order to bring about our genuine obedience and spirituality.

INTO HIS ARMS

In Hebrews 8:6 (and also in 9:15), Jesus Christ is described as the "Mediator" of the new and better covenant. Back in the messianic prophecies of Isaiah 42:6 and

disobey these laws was to *"break My covenant"* (Leviticus 26:15).

But even then God warned Moses that the people would fail at this: *"They will forsake Me and break My covenant* which I have made with them.... When I have brought them to the land flowing with milk and honey, of which I swore to their fathers, and they have eaten and filled themselves and grown fat, then they will turn to other gods and serve them; and *they will provoke Me and break My covenant"* (Deuteronomy 31:16-20).

Centuries later, God reminded the prophet Jeremiah of what His people had done through their chronic disobedience: "The house of Israel and the house of Judah have *broken My covenant* which I made with their fathers" (Jeremiah 11:10).

And in Isaiah 24:5, God extended this verdict of covenant-breaking to all mankind: *"The earth is defiled by its people; they have disobeyed the laws, violated the statutes and broken the everlasting covenant"* (NIV).

49:8, the Lord God had promised that He would give Christ "as a covenant to the people"—Christ Himself would *be* the covenant.

(Priest, messenger)

8. To better understand Christ's role in the New Covenant, look up Hebrews 7:22 and Malachi 3:1, which give other titles to Christ in reference to this covenant. "All these names," wrote Andrew Murray, "point to the one truth: that in the New Covenant, Christ is all in all." Record what these titles are, and add your thoughts on the significance of each.

Priest → King + Spiritual Ruler

Messenger → Of the Good News

As believers, you and I have been delivered out of the arms of the law and into the arms of Christ. As Paul expressed it, you died to the law "that you may be married to another—to Him who was raised from the dead" (Romans 7:4).

What a wondrous reality! Life is no longer to be lived under a code but through a Person, a breathtakingly glorious Person who is not only the unrivaled Sovereign of the universe but also the supreme Lover of our souls, One who infuses us moment by moment with resurrection power. The Old Covenant provided a code to live under; the New Covenant provides *a Person to live through.*

God's foremost calling for your life is a passionate and deepening love affair with His Son. When this is in place, God's standards will take care of themselves.

David Brainerd, the young eighteenth-century American missionary to the Delaware and Seneca tribes, discovered this powerfully in his preaching. He wrote,

"Ever since my first coming among these Indians" he had been "favored…in preaching Christ crucified, and making Him the center and mark to which all my discourses among them were directed.… And God was pleased to give these divine truths such a powerful influence…the precepts of morality, and spending time in repeated harangues upon external duties."

By contrast, being married to the law inevitably leads to despair. It's like living with Mr. Perfect. He never makes a mistake, never has a bad day, never indulges himself; he's always on time and on target in everything he does. Beyond this, he expects exactly the same from you. Perfection is your only acceptable standard, and he lets you know it every time you fail to measure up. If you do nine out of ten things right, you're still a failure.

Moreover, if you dare ask for his help in accomplishing the lists of responsibilities he keeps handing you, he turns a cold shoulder and tells you to try harder. It's all up to you. You feel an abiding sense of hopelessness.

How blessedly different is life married to our Lord! Instead of acceptance conditioned wholly by your performance, He assures you that you can never lose His love and provides you with an eternally significant purpose for living. He actually delights in you, and though He's displeased when you sin, this can never, ever cause Him to reject you. He sympathizes with your weaknesses and picks you up when you fall. Anything He asks you to do for Him, He Himself fully intends to do through you.

As Blaise Pascal expressed it, "The law demands what it cannot give; grace gives all it demands." No longer are we governed externally by a list of moral duties; we're now compelled internally to a lifestyle of radical, holy love because of the Person who's taken up residence within.

Of course many of the things your new Husband requires of you are the same things your former husband (the law) required, but now you do them freely, gladly, and even better than before. Grace always motivates and enables far beyond what law can do.

LOCATION, LOCATION, LOCATION

9. Regarding where God's law is "written," what primary difference do you see between the Old Covenant (look at Exodus 32:15-16) and the New Covenant (see Jeremiah 31:33)? And what does this difference fully mean for believers today? *With the old covenant the Lord wrote the law on stone tablets in the new covenant. He wrote the law on their mind & heart. The law of the covenant now lives in us.*

Under the law, God's commands were *externally imposed*—written on tablets of stone and given to Israel with the requirement for wholehearted obedience.

But in the New Covenant, God's commands are now *internally implanted*—inscribed within us, just as God promised through His prophets: "I will put My law *in their minds,* and write it *on their hearts*" (Jeremiah 31:33).

THE DESIRE IS THERE

What this startling truth means practically is that at the moment of your rebirth, God gave you a new set of godly inclinations, a divinely implanted disposition that always delights in doing His will. There is within you a Spirit-wrought disposition

> "We receive an inward fervency and light, whereby we are changed and become new creatures; whereby also we receive a new judgment, a new feeling, and a new moving. This change, and this new judgment, is no work of reason, or of the power of man, but is the gift and operation of the Holy Ghost, who comes...and brings forth in us spiritual motions."
>
> —Martin Luther

toward righteousness that can never be extinguished or diluted, though it can be submerged beneath other competing passions. *Within every believer, the desire to do the will of God is the gift of God.* This desire is not something to try and conjure up, but something already there, needing only to be nourished and appropriated.

10. Regarding the presence of God's Spirit, what primary change do you see promised in the New Covenant (look at Ezekiel 36:27 and John 14:16-17)? What significance does this have for us today? *In Ezekiel, the Lord talks about putting His Spirit in us so that we would obey His commands. In John, He tells us that the Holy Spirit will never leave us — only those who recognize the Holy Spirit who already lives w/ us.*

The desire to do God's will is within every believer because the Holy Spirit now dwells there. Normative Christianity is a blatantly supernatural affair, a life utterly dependent upon indwelling <u>resurrection power</u> from beginning to end. *The Old Covenant is man demonstrating what he can do for God; the New Covenant is God demonstrating what He can do for and through man.*

We could further define it in this way: The New Covenant is a radically *different* and radically *better* arrangement between God and His people, one that allows Him to accomplish in and through us what we're fundamentally incapable of doing under the law. It is God's <u>"I will"</u> overcoming our own <u>"I can't."</u>

THE HOLY SPIRIT IN THE OLD TESTAMENT

In the Old Testament, the Spirit of God rested "upon" various individuals, but not within them (in the New Testament sense). He was upon them temporarily but not permanently. (See Exodus 35:30-31; Deuteronomy 34:9; Judges 3:10; 11:29; 14:6,19; 15:14; 1 Samuel 11:6.)

OBEDIENCE NEW AND TRUE

11. One of the central passages in Scripture concerning the Christian's relationship to the law is Romans 7:1-6. Ponder this rich text, then answer the following questions.

(a) In verses 1-3, Paul used a couple's marriage bond as an illustration of the law. What was his point in making this comparison?

To show that a widow or widower isn't bond by the laws of marriage if their spouse were to die. They can remarry if they wish to + they wouldn't be breaking any laws because their spouse is dead.

(b) From that comparison, Paul then went on in verse 4 to define our present relationship (as Christians) to the law. What is that relationship to the law? And what does this mean practically and personally to you?

The law no longer holds me in its power, because I died to its power when I died w/ Christ. As a result I can produce good deeds because I want to now that His spirit lives in me, not because I have to.

(c) Continuing in verse 4 and on through verses 5 and 6, Paul then expressed the utterly profound effect this now has upon us. What are we now free to do? (List everything you can find in these verses.) ·

When controlled by my old sinful nature, old sinful desires were aroused in me, + the law would arouse these evil desires resulting in death— I was dying inside But now I've been born again in Christ + no longer bond by the law.

24

While we're free from the law in the New Covenant, we are *not* free from obedience. Paul alluringly pictured this obedience in surprising ways.

He likened it, for example, to childbearing. You're married to Christ "that [you] should bear fruit to God" (Romans 7:4; fruit is often a metaphor for children in Scripture). What an enticing portrait! Our obedience is simply the by-product of being impregnated with Christ, the tangible evidence of the divinely implanted life within us. *True obedience is not gritting our teeth and "doing the right thing"; it is cooperating with the breaking forth of Christ's life from within.* This fruit we bear as "children" to Christ includes not only new converts but also our godly character, good works, and worship.

Another image from Paul of our obedience is that of serving—"we should serve in the newness [freshness] of the Spirit and not in the oldness of the letter [the law]" (Romans 7:6). There is service for God that is musty-smelling, drab, lifeless. That's Old Covenant serving. But there's also a kind of ministry that has a fresh scent about it, one that exudes life and vitality. This is New Covenant serving, and with it "the fragrance of Christ" and "the aroma of life" (2 Corinthians 2:15-16) are unmistakably present.

AWAITING RELEASE

The writer of Hebrews saluted the New Covenant as "a better covenant" than the law because it is "established on better promises" and brings in "a better hope" (Hebrews 7:22; 8:6; 7:19). Even so, it's amazing to see how quickly we gravitate back to the old.

We see this in popular approaches to spiritual maturity among the Christian community today. In his book *Connecting,* Larry Crabb identifies a couple of these.

The first he calls the *"Do what is right"* approach. This is the moralistic model and insists that people simply need to be exhorted to do what the Bible says. Change comes as people repent—turning away from the wrong and doggedly pursuing the right. Particularly among fundamental, conservative evangelicals, this course is widely followed. At its core, it's an Old Covenant attempt at sanctification.

The second approach he describes as *"Fix what is wrong."* This is the therapeutic model, which says people can't do what's right until damage from the past is looked at and healed. Change comes as people are repaired, namely by getting in touch with what's going on inside of them, facing their pain and disappointments, and courageously moving forward. Doing this requires help outside the gospel.

Clearly there are elements of truth in both models, for the gospel calls us both to do what is right and to fix what is wrong. In both these systems, however, the means for change overlooks or denies the spiritual realities of the New Covenant in the life of the believer.

I would add yet another popular approach to this list, which could be called *"Get what is missing."* This is the power encounter model. It continually seeks miraculous experiences with God as the key to spiritual growth. Again there's clearly an element of truth here. We're indeed called to seek all God has for us and to mightily pursue His best. But how do we define God's best? A faith that requires an ongoing diet of signs and wonders will never mature properly.

A better model is what Larry Crabb calls *"Release what is good."* This is the very heartbeat of New Covenant spirituality. Because of the New Covenant, there are supernatural resources permanently residing within the soul of every believer, and they're the source of all spiritual good. Whatever "good" God wants to channel through us has *already* been placed within us; it simply awaits release.

This is what Jesus was alluding to when He promised, "He who believes in Me, as the Scripture has said, out of his heart will flow rivers of living water" (John 7:38). We're to allow the good (living water) to be released in a constant flow.

OUT OF HIDING

Charles Spurgeon tells the story of a minister in the north of England who felt led to give a sizable sum to a very poor woman in his congregation. He took the money and went to her house. He knocked several times at her door; there was no answer.

Later he met her at church and told her he had come by.

"When?" she asked.

After he told her the time of his visit, she confessed she actually had been home; she thought he was a bill collector, and having no means to pay, she hid in her room. It was the pastor's joy to let the woman know his visit was to give her money, not take it away.

Many Christians respond to God in just the same fashion. They see Him mainly as the moral bill collector of the universe, knocking on the door of their life to demand the obedience that is due Him. Yet they sense within themselves such limited resources that they despair of ever being able to comply with His commands. Overwhelmed by guilt and frustration, they eventually run away from His voice rather than toward it.

The truth is that God comes to us *first* to give and only afterward to receive. Certainly He requires of us a lifestyle that honors His name; our obedience is His rightful due. But He never requires anything *from* us that He hasn't already deposited *within* us.

Let me say again: *God requires from us only what He has already placed within us.*

We're called to let His living waters flow, to release what is good. This "good" is the full assortment of supernatural resources that were permanently implanted within you the instant you were born again and that are ready for release every day of your life on earth. In the heart of this workbook we'll explore in depth the four primary New Covenant provisions. My prayer is that as you discover more about them, releasing them will become easier indeed.

But to best understand and prepare for the most effective release of these provisions, we'll look first at their highest purpose, one that may be a surprise to you. Then we'll take a short but essential journey into a darkness that's absolutely necessary for gratefully and passionately appreciating the bright lights of the New Covenant.

Meanwhile, let me first invite you to pause and carefully consider your own life:

12. In what aspects of your life do you sense a genuine hunger for greater freedom and the release of greater spiritual power? *In the area of self control vs. God control. Truly releasing all my cares and worries over to Him & stop pondering over them. In the area of forgiveness, forgiving others as He has forgiven me.*

13. In what ways could it be possible that you've been hindered in your Christian life by an unrecognized law-based or legalistic approach to spirituality? *By the law itself - when it states that we have to forgive + because They're my in-laws I have to love + accept them either one right now. I have no desire to do*

OPTIONAL FURTHER STUDY (FOR GOING IN-DEPTH)—WHY THE LAW?

What was the fundamental purpose behind God's giving of the law?

The law wasn't given chiefly to regulate our daily lives, but to expose our desperate need. God's primary (though not only) intent behind loading us down with His righteous standards was to drive us into the arms of Christ both for justification and sanctification.

When we truly begin understanding what God is requiring of us and then set out to try and fulfill those requirements, it doesn't take long before the sheer weight of those demands causes us to totter beneath their weight. Only then are we ready to let Christ fulfill those standards for us. When this happens, the law has fulfilled its purpose within us.

1. Carefully explore enough of the following key passages from Deuteronomy to form thorough answers to these questions (and record your findings below): Deuteronomy 4:1-8,40; 5:28-33; 6:1-9,17-19,24-25; 8:1-20; 11:8-21; 30:17-20

(a) From what God told the people of Israel, how closely and completely would their experience of God's blessing be tied to their obeying His law?

(b) What do these verses indicate about the purpose of God's law?

(c) What else do you learn about God's law from these verses?

2. From the key passage of Galatians 3:19-25, what reasons can you find for why the law was given? (You may want to explore Christ's words and actions in Luke 24:27 and John 5:39 and Paul's words in Colossians 2:16-17.)

3. *From the key passage of Romans 7:5-13, how would you describe both the purpose and the effects of the law?*

4. *Why was the law unable to produce righteousness in us, according to Romans 8:3? (Explain this in your own words, to the best of your understanding.)*

5. *How should we understand Christ's relation to the law, according to His words in Matthew 5:17-18? And what does that mean for us, according to Paul's words in Romans 8:3-4 and 10:4?*

6. *And finally, how would you summarize the New Testament truth that brings together the law, Christ, and our faith, as Paul presented it in Galatians 3:10-14?*

First Things First: A Reputation at Stake

Put first things first and we get second things thrown in; put second things first and we lose both first and second things.

C. S. LEWIS

As our new church building was being constructed I observed an interesting phenomenon. Everything built first—the support for all else to come—disappeared from sight long before the project was completed. The foundation I'd seen being poured into place, the huge steel girders I'd watched being erected above that—all this was eventually hidden by things like walls and windows and floors and ceilings.

Of course I knew this would happen. In fact, I was impatient for such progress, eager to see the building's more practical aspects installed—the features we would continue seeing and touching and using after moving in.

But what if the construction workers had skimped on those beginnings? Suppose they'd rushed too quickly through the substructure stages to get to the "good" stuff that's more visible and practical? The answer is that the building, if standing at all, would be unstable and unsafe.

I believe the same is true in constructing our best understanding of a life in Christ that soars like an eagle. Getting to the "good" stuff—the practical teaching we can most easily see and touch and use—requires first the right foundation of good theology.

That's why it's time in our fresh look at supernatural living to set a solid biblical foundation. If we're to make the radical adjustments required by New Covenant spirituality, we have to be absolutely convinced that these changes are called for by nothing less than the Word of God. "First things first" is as trustworthy an approach here as anywhere.

In this week's lesson, we'll seek to understand more fully what the glory of God is, why it matters so much, and what significance it has for our New Covenant living.

1. How would you answer these questions, according to your best understanding at this time?

(a) What matters most to God?

That I truly love Him w/ all my heart mind & soul by the way I line my life & treat others.

(b) What cause is God most passionate about?

Loving Him + loving others enough to enable them to share in the kingdom.

(c) What is the primary reason God wants us to spread His gospel?

To make diciples so that everyone can line w/ Him in Heaven.

IS GOD ON YOUR SIDE?

So what exactly is "first" from God's viewpoint, according to His Word? What matters most to Him? What cause or issue is He most passionate about?

Early in America's Civil War a supporter of President Abraham Lincoln said to him, "I sure hope the Lord is on the side of the North." Lincoln thought a moment, then responded, "About that I am not at all concerned, but only that we should be on the side of the Lord."

That exchange illustrates much of what ails the modern church. More often than not, Christianity today is marketed to the church and to the world as the best way to get the good Lord on your side, the sure path to getting the finest help available, namely God's. A casual look around the average Christian bookstore reveals a sizable percentage of books that basically focus on how to *use* God. Their message is clear and predictable: God is absolutely essential for making your life work; for success in finances, family, health, holiness, politics, and personal fulfillment, your approach must include God and His principles.

But a deeper reality seems all but forgotten: The main point of our spirituality, according to the Bible, is the *furthering of God's glory,* not the fixing of our lives. In other words, *God does not exist for us; we exist for Him.*

So the question isn't whether God is on our side, responsive to our call, but whether we are genuinely on His side, responsive to His call. It isn't how God fits into what we're doing, but how we fit into what God is doing. He is the Creator; we are the creatures. He is the Sovereign; we are the subjects. He is the Master; we are the slaves. He runs the universe; we fit in.

Sin, however, has introduced the insane proposition that we can alter or even reverse these roles. If God cannot be dismissed, at least He can be utilized. The bumper-sticker slogan speaks for many: "God Is My Copilot." We supposedly honor God by extending to Him a place in the cockpit of our lives, inviting His input on how we can fly smoothly and successfully through life, and of course turning to Him in any emergency cases. But the true and living God is no one's copilot. He's in absolute and sole control of where we're headed and solicits no one's advice on how to get there. In all our lives, He relentlessly pushes forward His own kingdom agenda to its inevitable, glorious conclusion.

2. Based on what you know of Scripture, how fully do you agree with the points made in the preceding paragraphs? What questions or thoughts come to your mind about these points?

I completely agree. Many times we/I try to fit God into "my" life or "my" plan, when I forget that He's in total control of everything + I need to follow His leads be in His will.

WHAT MATTERS MOST

From Genesis to Revelation we discover that God has one central purpose for creation and humankind. This is stated in various ways, but it all comes down to one main issue—His glory.

Nothing—*nothing*—matters more to God than the glory of His name. He is ablaze with a perfect, pure jealousy for His reputation.

> A. W. Tozer speaks of the "Utilitarian Christ" that Christians tend to imagine and promote: "He is often recommended as a wonderfully obliging but not too discriminating big brother who delights to help us accomplish our ends, and who further favors us by forbearing to ask any embarrassing questions about the moral and spiritual qualities of those ends."

3. What did God tell Moses in Leviticus 10:3 and in Numbers 14:21?

"I will show myself Holy among those who are near me. I will be glorified before all the people." "But as surely as I live, & as surely as the earth is filled w/ God's glory, not one of these shall enter the land."

4. In God's reckoning, failure to acknowledge His glory constitutes a capital offense, not the mere misdemeanor we would prefer to make it. In Romans 1:21, what did Paul give as the ultimate reason for God's wrath against sinful mankind? *They wouldn't worship Him as God or even give Him thanks.*

Because of failure to glorify God, Moses missed the Promised Land, Aaron's two oldest sons were killed, Nebuchadnezzar was made to live like an animal, and Herod was eaten by worms (Numbers 20:12; Leviticus 10:1-3; Daniel 4:32-33; Acts 12:21-23). And so it goes throughout Scripture. One simply cannot escape the white-hot jealousy God has for His name and His glory.

GOD'S NAME

In Scripture, the phrase "name of God" contains three primary aspects.

It can be used in the sense of *character*—what He's like as a person. "For thus says the High and Lofty One who inhabits eternity, *whose name is Holy*" (Isaiah 57:15).

The phrase can also speak of His *reputation* or fame. "You showed signs and wonders against Pharaoh.... So *You made a name for Yourself,* as it is this day" (Nehemiah 9:10).

The phrase can also be used to highlight God's *authority*. "Lord, even the demons are subject to us *in Your name*" (Luke 10:17).

---

5. Even our salvation has more to do with the acclaim it brings to God than the good it brings to us. When Paul begins in Ephesians to speak so upliftingly of our salvation in Christ he repeatedly points us to the purpose behind it. What is that purpose, according to verses 6, 12, and 14 in Ephesians 1? *His kindness is praised for having us belong to His loving Son. To praise His Name. He has purchased us to be His own people.*

The most significant thing about your salvation and mine is the adoration and honor it brings to God. In the same way, our ministry is important not primarily for how it blesses others, but for the recognition and renown it brings to God.

6. (a) In 1 Peter 4:11, what reason did Peter give us for using our gifts in ministry to one another? *To give God glory in everything we do through Jesus Christ.*

(b) What, therefore, would you say is the ultimate test of whether our ministry is a "success"?
Whether or not it's glorifying God — not ourselves.

"*Whatever* you do, do all *to the glory of God*" (1 Corinthians 10:31). Our lives—together in the body of Christ as well as individually—must find their first and greatest significance in how they enhance God's reputation. This is our primary calling, the very purpose for our existence.

HEAVY AND SPECTACULAR

So what exactly is this "glory" of God?

I like to call it His "spectacularness." His glory is His stunning radiance, the overwhelming splendor of His excellence, His incomparable and exquisite beauty. The Hebrew term for "glory" comes from a root meaning "heavy" or "weighty." God's *glory* carries the full weight of all His attributes. The Bible likens that glory to images such as blinding light, raging fire, crashing thunder, flashing lightning, and a magnificent rainbow. Whatever else it may be, one thing is for sure—God's glory is awesome in appearance. It's too spectacular a sight to pass by without taking notice.

And He *wants* everyone to notice.

God's reputation has always been the whole point of human history and His foremost objective in choosing and blessing a people of His own. Through the prophet Isaiah we hear His voice calling out to "everyone who is called by My name, whom I have created *for My glory*"; we hear Him insisting, "This people I have formed for Myself; *they shall declare My praise*"; responding in prayer, Isaiah acknowledges, "You lead Your people, to make Yourself *a glorious name*" (Isaiah 43:7,21; 63:14).

God's utmost purpose for Israel was that they should spread His fame to surrounding nations. As the people of God lived out the commands of God, other nations would see His character fleshed out before them through acts of mercy, justice, and righteousness. Israel's visible lifestyle would spotlight the invisible yet mighty God who reigned over them and over the universe. In that small strip of land called Israel, the Lord would make clear on earth what has always been known in heaven—that He alone is God and is more than worthy of people abandoning themselves to Him in joyous worship and service.

7. How does the Bible portray God's glory? How does it reveal God's own attitude toward His glory, and what does it say our attitude should be?

For your meditation on those questions, choose some of the following passages and read them with an open mind and heart. Then record your thoughts in the space provided. (You may want to especially look for how God's glory is manifested in each case.)

Exodus 24:15-17; 33:18-23; 40:34-38; Numbers 14:20-24; Deuteronomy 4:34-38; 2 Chronicles 7:1-3; Psalm 29:1-9; Isaiah 40:5; Ezekiel 1:25-28; 39:21-24; 43:1-5; Habakkuk 3:3-6

God's Glory : A devouring fire, No one may see Him & live, a glorious cloud

His attitude : No one could see Him & live, We live for His glory & praise.

Our attitude : Adore & reverence Him, be loyal & obedient.

At Mount Sinai the Lord told His people, "You shall be to Me a kingdom of priests and a holy nation" (Exodus 19:6). As priests their role was to reflect God and dispense His Word to the rest of the world. As a holy nation, their character was in focus; they were to live as a "set apart" people, provoking those around them to seriously consider God as never before.

The Lord of heaven and earth was staking His reputation on the conduct of His children. Flesh-and-blood Israelites would serve as God's credentials, living proof that He alone is Lord. The spectacularness of God, the striking grandeur of God, would be seen through the most unlikely material of all—frail, faltering humanity. This is the essential meaning of what it is to glorify God.

STILL AT STAKE

As we move into the New Testament, we find striking parallels between Israel's calling and our own as members of Christ's body.

8. In imagery virtually identical to God's words at Sinai, Peter tells us (in 1 Peter 2:9), "You are a chosen generation, a royal priesthood, a holy nation, His own special people."

    Look up this verse. What did Peter go on to state as God's purpose for giving us this identity and status? *So that we could show others the goodness of God, For He called us out of darkness into His wonderful light.*

Once again God is staking His reputation on flesh and blood. As today's unbelievers observe God's children living in radical holiness, in supernatural community, and in overflowing grace, they too will be provoked to consider Christ in ways that a thousand tracts could never inspire.

"The first duty of the Christian," wrote John Calvin, "is to make the invisible kingdom visible." This can happen only when the divine resources of the New Covenant are unleashed in our lives.

WHERE GOD WAS BURIED

Unfortunately the Israelites failed tragically in their calling. Instead of glorifying His name—His character, His reputation, His authority—they did just the opposite. Through the prophet Ezekiel, God pronounced His indictment against them: "They profaned My holy name" (Ezekiel 36:20).

The Hebrew word translated as "profane" basically means "to treat as common or ordinary." Their lives had made God "ordinary." They had neutered God's reputation on earth. There was nothing in their conduct that elevated the name of their God over that of the many run-of-the-mill gods of their day. Certainly the Israelites claimed that He was the only true God, but nothing in their lifestyle required this claim be taken seriously.

This Hebrew word for "profane" can also be translated "to wound." In a real sense Israel wounded God's prestige; His name now limped among the nations.

Living with Impact

Early in 1871, a worldly, roving journalist named Henry Stanley headed into Africa's uncharted interior to find Dr. David Livingstone, the famous explorer and medical missionary who for years had been cut off from contact with Europeans. After finding Livingstone ten months later, Stanley went on to find something more, as he himself recounted:

"I went to Africa as prejudiced as the biggest atheist in London. But there came for me a long time of reflection. I saw this solitary old man there and asked myself, 'How on earth does he stop here—is he cracked, or what? What inspires him?' For months after we met I found myself wondering at the old man carrying out all that was said in the Bible—'Leave all things and follow Me.' But little by little his sympathy for others became contagious, my sympathy was aroused; seeing his piety, his gentleness, his zeal, his earnestness, and how he went about his business, I was converted by him, although he had not tried to do it."

Later Stanley wrote, "It wasn't Livingstone's preaching that converted me, it was his living."

This is what it means to serve as Christ's credentials: We live in such a way that people around us become intrigued with the reason behind it.

Let's look in detail at the passage from which this verse is taken.

9. Look up Ezekiel 36:16-27. As you investigate this passage, notice especially the charges God brings against His people, as a background for the New Covenant promises He makes.

(a) In what specific ways did the people of Israel "defile" their land, according to verses 17-18? Whom were these sins directed against?

By their evil deeds - murder, worshiping idols. These sins were directed against the Lord & His divine reputation.

(b) From what you see throughout this passage, how would you describe God's view of His name? What did His people fail to understand about His name?

He values His name very highly. That they dishonored His name by the way they lived in the sight of others. They didn't understand how holy His name was

(c) What does verse 23 indicate about God's ultimate purpose for the world (as well as the purpose behind His New Covenant promises, some of which are included in the passage beginning in verse 27)?

To show the world through His children's lives & behavior, how holy He is and will call Him Lord. To have His Spirit live in us so that we can easily obey Him.

How did Israel profane God's name?

Speaking through Ezekiel, God gave the answer: "I poured out My fury on them *for the blood they had shed* on the land, and *for their idols* with which they had defiled it" (Ezekiel 36:18). Their land was stained by *idolatry* and by *bloodshed.* God's two greatest commands for His people—to fully love God and to love one's neighbor as oneself—were being flagrantly violated.

Rather than giving God their undivided trust and adoration, Israel turned to the idols of the nations around them. And so they communicated a blatant message to all around: "God is not trustworthy enough or powerful enough to stake our lives upon. He doesn't come through. He just can't get the job done."

Besides their idolatry, God's people resorted to unrestrained selfishness instead of relating to one another in a way that reflected God's justice and love. Rampant hatred, to the point of bloodshed, replaced godly concern for one another.

They were no longer God's showcase. Instead, Israel in a sense had become His burial ground, for nothing about them gave convincing proof that the God who had parted the Red Sea was still alive.

The land of Israel had become like a beautiful wall spray-painted with ugly graffiti that blared two central messages: *God can't be trusted* and *People don't matter.*

IS GOD ENOUGH?

Is the same message blaring from God's people today?

The local church is where God is seeking to go public—not just a place where the gospel's truth is talked about, but where the gospel's attractiveness is visible. The local church, as Francis Schaeffer said, "should be right, but it should also be beautiful." It's through the community of Spirit-inhabited saints, more than any other way, that God intends to show the darkened world the kind of God He is.

Therefore, two chief callings rest upon us. The first is to live in such a way that our lives boldly proclaim, "There is only one God worthy of undivided trust and unrestrained adoration." The Bible calls this *faith*.

The second calling is to care for one another in such a way that unbelievers are amazed. The Scriptures call this *love*.

This combination is what puts God on display most noticeably before the world—our radical dependence on an unseen God plus our extraordinary concern for other people (especially fellow believers). Paul calls it "faith working through love" (Galatians 5:6).

Yet, like the Israelites of old, we can "defile the land." When we let other gods (money, career, approval, achievement, possessions, pornography, or whatever) meet our needs, we proclaim to all around, "God is not enough." And when we treat one another with indifference or disdain, when legalistic standards matter more than fellow saints, when church is more like a corporation than a family, we communicate to the world that people don't matter all that much.

The great tragedy and heinousness of our sin is not primarily the destruction it brings to our lives but the crippling it brings to God's name. Whenever a believer sins—whether it be the godless hedonism of license or the cold hardness of legalism—the worst result is that the glory of God is for that moment obscured; His name is made to limp. When our conduct nullifies our profession of God's greatness, when our lives fail to reflect the presence of resurrection power, we profane God's name.

THE MOST POWERFUL ARGUMENTS

Sheldon Vanauken captures a paradox:

"The best argument for Christianity is Christians; their joy, their certainty, their completeness. But the strongest argument against Christianity is also Christians—when they are somber and joyless, when they are narrow and repressive, then Christianity dies a thousand deaths."

To the Rescue

In the same passage from the prophet Ezekiel where God charged Israel with pro-faning His name and defiling the land, He confirmed also that He "had concern" (Ezekiel 36:21) for His holy name. The Hebrew word here means "to take pity upon" or "to have compassion toward." The same word is used of Pharaoh's daugh-ter having "compassion" (Exodus 2:6) when she found the baby Moses floating in a basket in the river, a compassion that caused her to rescue the child. As God saw His name lying wounded in Israel, He was stirred deeply to rescue it from further abuse.

How would He do it?

In this same chapter of Ezekiel, God sheds light on His promise of a New Covenant. "I will take you," He said;

> I will cleanse you from all your filthiness and from all your idols. I
> will give you a new heart and put a new spirit within you; I will
> take the heart of stone out of your flesh and give you a heart of
> flesh. I will put My Spirit within you and cause you to walk in My
> statutes. (Ezekiel 36:24-27)

In later lessons, we'll delve deeply into these incredible promises. But for now, consider *why* God was making them. "I do not do this," God said through Ezekiel, "for your sake, O house of Israel, *but for My holy name's sake,* which you have pro-faned" (Ezekiel 36:22). What spurred Him on to divine intervention was not the rescue of His people, *but the rescue of His name!*

God's controlling passion, His supreme concern, His unflinching priority is the grandeur and splendor of who He is. His matchless name may be scorned by the proud, blurred by those misrepresenting it, and yawned at by fools; but sooner or later God will come to its rescue.

And that rescue *will* succeed.

10. Examine the following passages. Summarize in your own words what they indicate about the "future" of God's glory.

Habakkuk 2:14; Matthew 24:29-30; 25:31-32; 1 Corinthians 15:24-28; Philippians 2:9-11; Revelation 21:22-27

A time will come where the earth will be filled w/ the glory of God. The Son of man will arrive on the clouds of heaven w/ power & great glory. When the Son of man comes in His glory, He will sit upon His glorious throne. Christ will reign over everything – God has given Him authority over all things. God Raised Jesus to the height of heaven so that every knee shall bow & call Him Lord.

God is not merely hoping or wishing that someday we'll give Him His due. He's ensuring it by active pursuit, steering all history toward that day when every knee will bow and every tongue confess "that Jesus Christ is Lord, *to the glory of God the Father*" (Philippians 2:10-11). In His own timing and by His own means He will continue to set high over all peoples and nations that infinite glory belonging to His name alone. Already, this very moment, He is harvesting His glory from among the nations through the spread of His gospel and the worship and testimony of His people.

To be sure, the global conquest of God's glory will not fully occur until Christ Himself personally returns to set up His kingdom. In the meantime, you and I are part of a community whose central purpose is to participate with God in His relentless march toward seeing His name rightly exalted.

SURPRISED? OFFENDED?

All this is *not* to say that people don't matter to God. He created us, He pursues us, He provides for us, He even died for us. The whole of Scripture testifies to the wondrous reality of His unfathomable love toward us. *We matter much to God…but we don't matter most.* We can't and we shouldn't. *(i.e. our kids vs. God's attention)*

You see, an infinitely perfect God must supremely value that which *is* of supreme value. If He doesn't, He's no longer perfect. If God were to value people over His name, the inversion would disqualify Him from being God.

Yet so many Christians are surprised or even offended to be told that what counts most to God is His glory, not us. Many of us have grown up all our lives hearing that *we* rank first to God, because of His love. But this cannot be true, as we'll continue to discover in very practical terms. And precisely because it isn't true, our highest well-being is assured.

11. How do you respond to the statement above that we are *not* what matters most to God? How fully do you accept and believe this? Does it raise any doubts or questions in your mind?

I was somewhat surprised because of the depth of His love for us. But if He didn't value Himself as most important, I don't think He would have the supremacy and power that He has over the world & its people.

C. S. Lewis was right: "Put first things first and we get second things thrown in: put second things first and we lose both first and second things." When God is approached primarily as the great Fixer of life, with *our* needs as His prime agenda, our lives will not only fail to reflect His glory, but we'll also fail to experience change and fulfillment in the deepest, richest sense. When, however, we delight most in the spectacularness of God, when His glory becomes our highest agenda, we find a taste that thrills our souls plus a nonstop transformation in our lives along the way.

12. In light of the issues raised in this lesson, how might you have been viewing God inadequately?

As His ultimate goal & purpose was to love me & fill me w/ His joy, where now I realize that that is secondary to Him.

OPTIONAL FURTHER STUDY (FOR GOING IN-DEPTH)—HIS GLORY AND OUR GLORY

1. *Our understanding of God's glory explodes into a new dimension as we see how Jesus revealed His Father's glory. Explore some of the following passages, and let them awaken your thoughts. Then summarize what we can learn about God's glory through Christ.*

    Matthew 17:1-2; Luke 2:9-14; John 1:14; 2:11; 8:54; 11:39-44; 12:23-29; 17:1-5; 2 Corinthians 4:3-6; Revelation 5:11-14

2. *Notice in the following passages how the people of God are intimately involved in God's glory (or "splendor" or "honor"). How exactly is this possible? What does it mean for us? Choose some of these passages for your study and meditation, and record your observations and reflections.*

    Isaiah 46:12-13; 60:1-3; 62:1-3; Jeremiah 33:7-9; John 15:7-8; 17:10; Romans 5:2; 8:18; 15:7; Colossians 3:4; 1 Thessalonians 2:12; 1 Peter 4:14; Revelation 21:9-11

Becoming Spiritually Provocative

Preach the gospel at all times. If necessary, use words.

FRANCIS OF ASSISI

I have a pair of sunglasses I especially like. I don't know exactly what kind of special tinting the lenses have, but it sure changes the way everything looks. Greens are greener, yellows are brighter—every color seems a bit more vivid. In fact, I hate to take them off.

When the glory of God takes possession of us, it's very much like wearing those sunglasses. Everything looks different! There's a new vividness to life, a heightening of purpose, a clarity of focus, and a vibrancy of spirit that belong only to those held captive by His glory. Moreover, we'll joyously embrace God's goal for our lives to make us not just spiritually *whole* but spiritually *provocative*.

God's highest agenda for our lives is not that they be simply good, moral, and responsible, but that they be spiritually intriguing, even mystifying. God wants us "conformed to the image of His Son" (Romans 8:29), as Paul said, and a Christlike life is one that puzzles, attracts, disrupts, entices, enrages, comforts, rebukes, and, most of all, radically loves those around it. It's a life that will provoke others to a new contemplation of God.

So the central issue is not what kind of obedience will prompt God into making our life more manageable and successful, but what kind of obedience will make God's excellence more visible on the playing field of life. What *specifically* does such obedience look like for you and for me?

In this week's lesson we'll explore the practical and transforming implications of God's glory for our lives and what we need in order to display God's glory.

UNIQUE APPLICATIONS

When John the Baptist was in the wilderness preaching about repentance to huge crowds, they asked him, "What shall we do?"

John could have answered with a generalized "Love God and do what is right." But he was much more specific.

1. Explore this incident with John the Baptist as narrated in Luke 3:10-14.
   In verse 11, how did John answer the people's question? Write his response here:

This challenging answer was designed to promote both *radical trust in an unseen God* and *genuine concern for others' needs.* As the people gave away their extra to those in need, they demonstrated that their trust was not in any surplus but in a faithful God.

John was later approached by a group of tax collectors and then by a band of soldiers—two sets of people quite different from one another and from the crowd at large. Like the larger crowd, both the tax collectors and the soldiers asked John separately, "What shall we do?"

Again John could have responded with a generic answer, or at least the same response he gave earlier. Instead he carefully crafted applications that were unique to each group.

2. How did John answer the tax collectors (in verse 13)?

3. How did he answer the soldiers (in verse 14)?

Why did he answer each group so differently? Because each group had a distinctive sphere of influence and therefore its own opportunity *to unleash the glory of God* in that sphere. He asked both the tax collectors and the soldiers to do what was almost unheard of in that day. (Tax collectors who taxed fairly and soldiers who didn't bully or bribe would get everybody's attention.) The same unexpectedness was true of the answer he gave in verse 11 to those who first asked him.

Three groups…three separate answers. In each case the questioners were asked to approach life in a radically different manner than what was normal, enabling them to shake up people's perspectives on God.

The bottom line for all of us: *Give others a clearer glimpse of God.*

WHAT SHALL WE DO?

That's also the bottom line for us.

I encourage you to ask yourself, What does focusing first on God's glory look like in every area of my life?

4. *(This may be a good time to pause briefly and ask for the Holy Spirit's help in understanding His truth for you in this week's lesson.)* Reflect on what

focusing first on God's glory could look like specifically in *your work.* Envision it as fully as you can. Record your thoughts here:

Do we see our work primarily as a place to earn a paycheck or advance our career? Paul taught workers in their labor to "adorn the doctrine of God our Savior in all things" (Titus 2:10). With a view to that kind of "adornment"—God's glory—we learn to see the marketplace first and foremost as an arena for displaying the light of the gospel.

That's why there's no such thing as an "ordinary" job. Every task done for God's glory is of eternal significance.

5. Now envision what focusing first on God's glory would look like in *how you relate to those in authority over you.* Record your thoughts here:

How do we respond to authority? Do we show respect and submission mainly because it keeps us out of trouble? When our aim is to glorify God, true respect and submission signal to the world our confidence in One who's infinitely greater than any human authority. Peter says this is one of the ways unbelievers will be impacted so that they "glorify God in the day of visitation" (1 Peter 2:12)—the day God draws near to them.

6. How would focusing first on God's glory impact *your marriage?* Reflect on this, and record your thoughts here:

As a husband and wife learn to glorify God and allow themselves to be Spirit-dominated, they see their relationship not as a filling station for their own needs but a way to clearly reflect resurrection power. When their needs are unmet by one another, they're able to view it not as a blockade to happiness but as an opportunity for supernatural responding, thereby increasing glory for God.

7. What difference could you foresee in *your prayer life* from fully focusing on God's glory?

When God's name and interests are paramount, our prayer is not, "Our Father who art in heaven, please bankroll the needs I'm about to tell You," but rather, "Hallowed be Your name. Your kingdom come. Your will be done on earth as it is in heaven" (Matthew 6:9-10). His name and His kingdom receive top billing in our petitions, before we move to personal needs.

FOR OUR CHILDREN

Perhaps you're a parent. What will a focus on God's glory mean for you in that arena?

8. What difference could you foresee in *your parenting* from fully focusing on God's glory?

The prophet Malachi tells us that the Lord "seeks godly offspring" (Malachi 2:15) from our marriages. His design for our children (as for all of us) is that they be not merely well-adjusted, contributing members of society, but living dispensers of His spectacularness wherever He stations them on this earth.

As I consider my three sons, this perspective has tremendous ramifications. When I think about them, pray for them, and relate to them, I must do so transcendently. I must realize there's something at stake in their lives far greater than their own well-being and comfort, something that surpasses all the pleasures and heartaches earth has to offer.

What do I want for them? Is it good grades, a good college, a satisfying job, a good marriage, a good family, involvement in a good church, and finally a secure retirement? Certainly I would enjoy seeing these things for each of my sons. But viewing them through the lens of God's glory requires me to see something greater.

What I want most is that they "max out" (to use their lingo) their unique potential for advancing God's reputation. These three men are "His workmanship, created in Christ Jesus for good works, which God prepared beforehand" (Ephesians 2:10). Whatever these preordained works are, whatever God's distinctive design is for each of my sons, it all centers on making His excellence known. What matters most is that they discover and participate in their God-crafted niche for shining forth His glory in this dark world. This alone will determine their true success.

Such a perspective has been critical for me in being able to deal with their disabilities. Two of my sons have significant learning disabilities; one is mildly affected by cerebral palsy. As I father them, I've been ministered to time and again by C. S. Lewis's statement, "Every disability conceals a vocation." It reminds me that God has an eternally significant purpose behind their disabilities, a distinct vocation for glorifying Him, something that transcends any other achievement.

This vocation may mean going to college…but it may not. At times it may mean a comfortable, secure job; it might also mean getting fired. It may mean a happy, fulfilling marriage, but there's no guarantee. It may mean raising their own children who love and serve God, or they may live with the heartache of a prodigal. The all-important issue is that, whatever circumstances God places them in, their lives are to display His spectacularness through their own unique design.

My parenting must be much more concerned with helping them hear and

TWO TRAINS

So we see that there are fundamentally two ways to approach our spiritual lives: Live for God, so that we can fully exploit His blessings; or live for Him so He can fully reveal His name.

A few years ago my wife and I took a train from New York City to New Haven, Connecticut. As we boarded the train in Grand Central Station I noticed another train right beside ours, one whose posted destination was a city hundreds of miles from New Haven. Both trains headed out in the same direction. Yet the farther we went, the greater divergence there was between the two. What began as identical directions ended up far, far apart.

A similar thing is happening today in the church. We're inviting people to board one of two trains for their spiritual journey.

The first is far and away the most popular. It says Christianity is primarily about God benefiting His creatures. This approach teaches that what matters most to God is people. Their well-being—

respond to God's call than simply getting them to conform to my standards of behavior. I must have big enough dreams and aspirations for them, dreams that go beyond happy, successful, respectable lives. If I can be used of the Spirit to help each one move toward his God-crafted niche and be increasingly caught up in the Lord's glory, I will have given them the greatest gift fatherhood has to offer.

MORE GLORY TO GOD

9. With an open mind and heart, explore some of the passages on the next page to find out more of how we can glorify God. How would you summarize the way these passages relate to your own experience and responsibilities?

spiritual, physical, and psychological—is what drives His actions and determines His priorities. Passengers on this train keep asking, "What must I do to gain God's blessing?"

"The church of North America has become so success oriented," writes Eugene Nida, "that we go from seminar to seminar on how to use God, but few are sitting in quiet holiness asking, 'How can God use me?' "

The second approach is less popular but far more biblical. It teaches that Christianity is primarily about God's glorifying His name. This is His core motivation for all He does. On this train, the passengers keep asking, "What can I do to better reflect God's glory?"

Early on, both these approaches look quite similar. But the farther one goes on life's journey, the more significant the difference becomes, especially in things like suffering, sacrifice, submission, prayer, and ministry.

John 14:13; 15:7-8; Acts 2:44-47; Romans 8:16-17; 15:7;
1 Corinthians 6:18-20; 1 Peter 1:6-7

SEE THE DIFFERENCE

10. Choose one or more of the following persons, then summarize (a) *in what way* the glory of God was made known to him in the passage listed and (b) how the experience of God's glory *affected* that person.

   Isaiah (in Isaiah 6:1-5); Ezekiel (in Ezekiel 1:26-28); John (in Revelation 1:13-17)

What practical difference will it make if we focus first on God's glory?
   The difference will show in our humility and personal brokenness.

> "The true way to be humble is not to stoop until you are smaller than
> yourself, but to stand at your real height against some higher nature
> that will show you what the real smallness of your greatness is."
>
> —Phillips Brooks

Early in Isaiah the prophet is pronouncing "woe" upon other people: "Woe to those who draw iniquity with cords of vanity.… Woe to those who call evil good, and good evil" (Isaiah 5:18,20). But in the very next chapter he sees "the Lord sitting on a throne, high and lifted up." In the blinding light of God's blazing holiness, Isaiah's "woe" turns inward: "Woe is *me,*" he cries, "for I am undone!" (Isaiah 6:1-5). He now recognizes that he isn't all that different from those he has just been condemning.

The air in a room appears clear until a sunbeam enters through a window. Then, in the light of that ray, you see countless particles of dust for the first time. In the same way, the depths of our sin remain hidden until seen in the light of God's holy excellence.

Truly confronting God's glory will also ignite a holy zeal within us for His name, as it did for young David when he shouted to Goliath, "I come to you *in the name of the LORD of hosts,* the God of the armies of Israel, whom you have defied" (1 Samuel 17:45).

Years later, the Son of David would do battle with the religious establishment of His day by making a whip and driving out "moneychangers" from the temple, overturning their tables and scattering their coins. What drove Jesus to such lengths? At the time, these actions caused His disciples to remember a prophecy in Scripture: "Zeal for Your house has eaten Me up" (John 2:13-17). It was fiery zeal for His Father's reputation that brought this astonishing outburst from Jesus.

Being absorbed with God's glory will also result in the purifying of our lives— so that we're "transformed," as Paul said, "from glory to glory." We can't transform ourselves, but God's Spirit accomplishes it, Paul explained, while we're "beholding as in a mirror the glory of the Lord" (2 Corinthians 3:18). To be transformed, our job is to "behold"—to continually contemplate—God's glory, focusing our spiritual gaze not primarily on things like Christian duties or our unworthiness, but on God's spectacularness.

11. Concentrate your thought on the truths presented in 2 Corinthians 3:17-18 and 4:6. Think deeply and personally about these passages. What can you expect to happen in your life as a result of these truths? What can you trust God for?

INGODDED PEOPLE

Nothing so invigorates our souls, so ravishes our hearts, so diminishes our anxieties, and so ennobles our existence as being supremely preoccupied with God's greatness and presence. This is what you and I were made for.

THE PROVOCATIVE DIFFERENCE

Focusing first on the glory of God means a paradigm shift of monumental proportions, one which will radically alter the way we approach everything and everyone.

When we're captivated by a genuinely Christian worldview (the joyous and tenacious belief that *the glory of God* is the supreme reality of the universe), we'll see all things in this new light. And this Christ-entranced perspective will ultimately be immensely practical in application.

The application, however, will have far more to do with advancing God's reputation than merely fixing our lives. We'll see that God's primary goal for us is to make us not just spiritually *whole*, but spiritually *provocative*.

That's why glorifying God and satisfying ourselves is a win-win proposition. As John Piper expressed it, "God's deepest commitment to be glorified and my deepest longing to be satisfied are not in conflict, but in fact find simultaneous consummation" when we glorify God. This is what Piper called "the wonder of the gospel" and the most freeing discovery he'd ever made.

But this supernatural outcome requires the unleashing of supernatural resources. For others to notice God in His people, there must be literally something of *Him* inside of us. That's why God, in the New Covenant, made His promise to invade and indwell us, creating a whole new society of "ingodded" (to use Dante's term) men and women.

This is as it must be—for our flesh is wholly incapable of pulling off the divine performance God has prepared us for. It takes nothing less than indwelling deity to override sin's power and display handiwork worthy of God's name. And nothing less is what God indeed has provided.

12. Think about your response to the statements made in the last few paragraphs.

    (a) Which of these thoughts and phrases carry the most weight for you?

    (b) What further questions or challenges or thoughts come to your mind?

13. How would you talk over with God what you've been impressed with in this week's lesson? Write your response here as a prayer to Him.

OPTIONAL FURTHER STUDY (FOR GOING IN-DEPTH)—EXPERIENCING GOD'S GLORY

1. *Use the richness and power of God's Word to help you spend a few quiet moments in reflection on God's glory. Let yourself be preoccupied with God's greatness and His presence—to invigorate your soul, ravish your heart, diminish your anxieties, and ennoble your existence.*

   Look up the following passages and find those that speak most directly to you. If the verses are familiar, revisit them in the fresh light of what you've learned so far in this workbook. Then record how these passages help you and edify you.

   1 Chronicles 29:10-13; Psalms 63:1-8; 108:3-5; 113:1-9; 145:1-21; Daniel 4:34-35; Ephesians 3:20-21; 1 Peter 5:10-11; Revelation 4:1-11

2. *Combine prayer with reflection on God's reputation as you make any of the following Scripture prayers your own. Ask the Holy Spirit to guide you in these moments of private worship. (You may want to write down your expressions of prayer in the space provided.)*

Deuteronomy 32:3-4; 2 Samuel 22:31-32; Job 36:26-33; 37:5-13; Psalms 66:3-4; 71:19; 86:8-9; 92:4-8; 93:1-5; 145:1-13

The Journey to Radical Dependence

What terrifies us is not the explosive force of the atomic bomb, but the power of the wickedness of the human heart.

ALBERT EINSTEIN

Years ago the children of a family vacationing on the Gulf Coast in Texas came across a soaked and scraggly little dog. Unable to find its owner, they prevailed upon their parents to take it home with them.

Back home, they washed and groomed their new pet. The next morning they left it alone in the house with food, water, and their pet cat. Returning later in the day, they discovered that their cat was deceased. Badly deceased in fact. It was also clear that their new pet was the culprit.

The following day the parents took the dog to the vet, thinking it wise to have it checked out. The vet informed them that the creature they'd taken in wasn't really a dog at all—it was an African rat. Apparently it had found its way ashore from an oceangoing ship docked along the coast.

A rat is a rat is a rat. It doesn't matter whether it's cleaned and groomed or dirty and scraggly, whether it lives in a sewer or a palace, whether it's cared for or shunned. Wherever it lives, whatever it looks like, however it smells, it will always be a rat.

The same is equally true concerning what the Bible calls our "flesh," that God-hostile, self-centered part of us often referred to as our "fallen nature" or "sin nature" or "carnal nature." Whether our flesh hangs out in church or at a bar, whether it's highly disciplined or self-indulgent, whether it's intoxicated by religious success or by alcoholic drink, it is still flesh. No matter how respectable it looks, how refined its manners, how religious its conduct, its fundamental nature remains unaltered. It is sin-riddled through and through, with no hope whatsoever of improvement.

That's why Jesus told his disciples, "The flesh profits nothing" (John 6:63). Notice He didn't say "little." The word is *nothing*. No amount of self-help, positive thinking, therapy, meditation, or discipline will ever improve this nature. It is flesh, will always be flesh, and will always have absolutely nothing to offer our spirituality.

We really don't believe this, however, and that could be our main problem as Christians.

This lesson's journey into darkness is not a pleasant one, but it's absolutely essential. By better understanding our inner devastation, we'll more quickly turn to a radical dependence upon God and His supernatural enablement.

1. "The flesh profits *nothing*"—that's what Jesus said. What recent evidence do you see in your own life of how much you either believe or don't believe those words?

A HEART PROBLEM, AND A HEART SOLUTION

2. (a) On a scale of 0 to 10, how would you rate the innate goodness of human beings?

(b) What average rating do you think other people in our society would give in answering that question?

Many decades ago a columnist in the *London Times* often ended his articles with the words, "What's wrong with the world?" According to a commonly told story, G. K. Chesterton finally sent in the following letter.

SWIM AND SINK—OR BE SAVED

If I were in the room with you now and tried handing you a life jacket, you probably would turn it down. At best you might politely hold it before setting it aside once I'd left.

If however we were on a sinking ship in the middle of the ocean, you would take hold of that same life jacket with a passion.

We're born into this world on a sinking ship, wholly enslaved to sin. God holds out a life jacket—the provisions of the New Covenant. But until we're convinced that our plight is truly desperate, we won't seize hold of God's offer.

Of course this is true first of all in our need to come to Christ for salvation. But after we're saved and continuing on in the Christian life, how many of us essentially take off the life jacket and try swimming again on our own?

Even as Christians, we won't flee to the supernatural resources provided only by God until all hope and confidence in our natural resources are shattered. "The end of ourselves," as someone put it, "is the beginning of God."

Dear Editor:

What's wrong with the world? I am.

    Faithfully yours,

    G. K. Chesterton

Chesterton understood the Bible's teaching on humanity's central problem: It's *us;* more specifically, it's what lies *in* us.

3. Look up Deuteronomy 5:24-29, where Moses recalled how the people responded at Mount Sinai when he was receiving the law from God.

(a) What confident assertion did the people make about themselves at the end of verse 27?

(b) What do you think prompted them to say this about themselves?

There's no hint of insincerity in the people's statement; they were fully resolved to do God's will—all of it. (How often have you and I done the same? We clearly hear the convicting voice of God in church, or at a retreat, or in a moment of quiet prayer…and with highest hopes and best intentions we promise that *we* will now make our lives different.)

4. Look at God's response to Moses (in verses 28-29) after hearing the people's statement.

(a) Summarize what the Lord said.

(b) What does this comment reveal about His love and concern for the people?

(c) In your own words, summarize the root problem experienced by the people of Israel, as well as the root problem experienced by all mankind.

God knew that the kind of "heart" necessary to obey Him was missing in every one of the people of Israel, as they themselves would quickly and tragically demonstrate. Forty years later, as the people prepared to finally enter the Promised Land, God gave them their first promise of the New Covenant: "The LORD your God will *circumcise your heart* and the heart of your descendants, to love the LORD your God *with all your heart*" (Deuteronomy 30:6).

MUD IN A SLUM

Heart is the word the Bible uses most often to describe the whole of our interior life. The heart is our "control central." In Scripture it refers to our intellect, to our emotions, to our will, and to our conscience.

Heart also refers to our spiritual yearnings. God has created us with deep cravings in our spirit especially for *relationship* and for *impact*. We hunger to be loved so relentlessly and unconditionally that we won't have to perform for acceptance. We also hunger to make an unerasable difference in our world, to leave an imprint from our lives that will never be washed away by the tide of time.

All five of these components of our heart—intellect, emotions, will, conscience, and spiritual longings—were created by God and are good in and of themselves. All five were to be used for glorifying Him. But all five have been badly warped because of the Fall.

Our mind was given to discover and ponder God's character and truth, but we've used it instead to produce and embrace poisonous philosophies and self-centered rationalizations. Our intellect has become "darkened" (Romans 1:21), to use the New Testament word. We don't think as God thinks. Our thoughts have become so clouded by innate sinfulness that we're incapable of God-honoring rationality.

Our emotions were given for loving God and others, but they've been degraded, "serving various lusts and pleasures" (Titus 3:3), as Paul said. We love what we should hate and hate what we should love.

Our will is God's wonderful gift for choosing and going in His direction, but it has become defiant instead. As Isaiah says, "We have turned, every one, to his own way" (Isaiah 53:6).

The conscience is our internal alarm system from God, to warn when moral danger is impending and to confirm when we're doing right. But our conscience has become defiled and is no longer reliable as a moral compass.

Finally, *our spiritual appetites* have become diverted to the point that Paul could say, "There is none who seeks after God" (Romans 3:11). These desires have not been extinguished, but rather rerouted; we drink spiritually at muddy watering holes to quench our thirst and eat from the city dump to satisfy our hunger. C. S. Lewis pictured our situation as "an ignorant child who wants to go on making mud pies in a slum because he cannot imagine what is meant by the offer of a holiday by the sea."

Ultimately all sin is taking one of these God-given longings and going in a God-absent direction to fulfill it. It's what God once pictured in these words: "My people have committed two evils: they have forsaken Me, the fountain of living waters, and hewn themselves cisterns—broken cisterns that can hold no water" (Jeremiah 2:13). George MacDonald was pointing to this when he made the daring assertion that when a man knocks at a brothel, he is really knocking for God.

In short, our hearts have become wholly infected by the cancer of sin. We're hopelessly short-circuited in our wiring for godly righteousness and joy.

Needless to say, this isn't our culture's prevailing view of ourselves. However, until we understand (as someone has observed) that in our fallen state we much more closely resemble Adolf Hitler than Jesus Christ, we don't yet grasp the Bible's take on humanity and sin.

"Through the whole of the Old Covenant there was always one trouble. Man's heart was not right with God. In the New Covenant the evil is to be remedied. Its central promise is a heart delighting in God's law and holding fellowship with Him."

—Andrew Murray

ARE WE *THAT* BAD?

But, come on, is our natural heart really *that* bad? Obviously we're fallen, but aren't words like *warped, darkened, degraded,* and *defiled* a bit harsh and exaggerated to describe our inner natures? And what about all the seemingly good people who aren't Christians but who do so much to help others and to better the world—are they really wicked, warped, defiled? The answer rests on our standard of measurement.

5. According to your present understanding, how would you answer the questions in the preceding paragraph?

The true standard for goodness and righteousness is given us by God. In fact, the standard *is* God. Without keeping this fact in focus, we remain naively optimistic concerning our own and others' moral capabilities.

We easily slip into a "street level" view of goodness. It's like walking down a city sidewalk and comparing the heights of those you pass by. A few people happen to be well over six feet tall and really stand out from the crowd. But if you were to look down on the same scene from atop a hundred-story skyscraper, everybody on the sidewalk would appear equally tiny.

When God looks down on all humanity from heaven, what's His assessment? The Bible speaks directly to this. "God looks down from heaven upon the children of men," David tells us, "to see if there are any who understand, who seek God." What does God find? "Every one of them has turned aside; they have together become corrupt; there is none who does good, no, not one" (Psalm 53:2-3).

Paul quoted that passage to the believers in Rome, introducing it with this sentence: "There is none righteous, no, not one" (Romans 3:10). Those words focus on our *internal disposition* toward sin. We're all unrighteous sinners by *nature.* And David's words—"there is none who *does* good, no, not one" (3:12)—focus on our *external actions* of sin. We're also sinners by *deed.* Our actions are tainted by the same dye of sin that permeates our fallen nature. That permeation is so complete that we find ourselves continually captivated by foolishness, inclined toward evil, and cold and unyielding toward God.

6. (a) Look at these passages, then summarize in your own words how they describe the characteristics of our natural heart.

   Genesis 8:21; Ecclesiastes 9:3; Jeremiah 17:9; Ephesians 4:17-18

(b) What are one or two ways in which you have seen these characteristics in your own experience?

SINS OF THE FLESH, SINS OF THE SPIRIT

In 2 Corinthians 7:1, Paul said we're to "cleanse ourselves from all filthiness of the *flesh* and *spirit.*"

Sins of the flesh are things like drunkenness, fornication, and stealing that violate God's moral standards for external holiness.

Sins of the spirit are things like pride, envy, and unforgiveness that violate His standards for internal holiness. This second category is as evil as the first, if not more so. Listen to C. S. Lewis again:

> The sins of the flesh are bad, but they are the least bad of all sins.
> All the worst pleasures are purely spiritual: the pleasure of putting
> other people in the wrong, of bossing and patronising and spoiling
> sport, and back-biting; the pleasures of power, of hatred. For there
> are two things inside me, competing with the human self which I
> must try to become. They are the animal self, and the Diabolical
> self. The Diabolical self is the worse of the two. That is why a cold,
> self-righteous prig who goes regularly to church may be far nearer to
> hell than a prostitute. But, of course, it is better to be neither.

7. Read the parable Jesus told in Luke 15:11-32 about the lost or "prodigal" son. What particular sins are in evidence in this story? Make a list of them here, and indicate who committed them.

In this parable, the younger brother's misdeeds were sins of the flesh. Meanwhile the failures of his older brother were sins of the spirit. Why did Jesus make this older son out to be a bad guy? After all, here was the epitome of responsibility and obedience.

The answer strikes home when we look at the situation in which Jesus told this story. Luke set the scene: "All the tax collectors and the sinners drew near to Him to hear Him. And the Pharisees and scribes complained, saying, 'This man receives sinners and eats with them'" (15:1-2).

We find two quite distinct groups hanging around Jesus. First are the easily recognized sinners of the day, tax collectors and the like (comparable to today's pimps, prostitutes, and drug dealers). They *knew* they were sinners and had little interest in religiosity, but they found Jesus wonderfully alluring (just as today's blatant "sinners" often do).

The other group was the well-camouflaged sinners—Pharisees and scribes, society's religious leaders (like some of today's preachers, deacons, Sunday-school teachers). They were thoroughly orthodox, doctrinally sound, and morally upright. They were also wholly unaware of their pervasive sinfulness.

In the story Jesus told on this occasion, the younger son—the "prodigal"—represented the tax collectors and sinners. Unencumbered by the restraints of religion and morality, their lives were characterized by wanton drinking and partying, cheating on taxes and on spouses, lying and stealing to get ahead. Here was *blatant disobedience* of God's standards—in other words, *sin.*

The older brother represented the Pharisees and scribes. Their lives were marked by slavish and joyless devotion to obedience and duty, by disciplined morality, grim piety, rigid law-keeping, smug superiority. Here was *counterfeit obedience* of God's standards—in other words, *sin.* They thought of unrighteousness only in terms of others' actions, such as lying or stealing, and missed the often greater unrighteousness of godless attitudes underlying their own "good" deeds.

In this vein, it's interesting to note the father's response to his older son's lack of inward righteousness. "Son," the father told him, "you are always with me, and all that I have is yours" (verse 31). In other words, "I myself, as well as all my provisions, are always with you; what more could you want?"

The same holds true for us all. Oswald Chambers wrote that the root of sin is unbelief in the goodness of God. Sin is every bit as much about distrust of God's heart and hand as it is about defiance of His standards. All sin ultimately makes its way back to our firmly rooted distrust of God and our desperate determination to find life on our own.

WHAT, WHY, HOW

Does all this mean it's impossible for any unbeliever, or any Christian relying on his own effort, to do anything good or righteous? Again, the answer depends on the standard of measurement.

8. How would you answer the question in the paragraph above?

God views our deeds from three angles through what I like to call His "trifocals." He scrutinizes not only *what* we do, but also *why* we do it and *how.*

He measures *what* we do by His directives in Scripture. To violate those directives is clearly sin, yet meeting this standard is more difficult than most of us realize. Jesus summarized the whole of God's mandate by saying we're to unreservedly

---

DRUNKEN PEASANTS

Martin Luther was exactly right: "The world resembles a drunken peasant; when you lift him into the saddle on one side, he tumbles off on the other."

All of us topple at times to the side of either legalism or license. In reference to Jesus' parable of the prodigal son, our flesh erupts in either the younger son's blatant disobedience or the older son's counterfeit obedience.

Personally, I know I've come to see more of that older brother in me than I ever cared to know.

---

love God and to love our neighbor as ourselves (Mark 12:28-31). The standard is simply a life wholly abandoned to perfect loving! (This is why the litmus test for how we're doing spiritually is not the Ten Commandments, but 1 Corinthians 13.) To meet this standard requires that we spend every waking moment of our existence in loving God and others perfectly. Moreover, Christ gave this mandate an internal dimension, showing us by way of example that unresolved anger and hatred toward someone will incur judgment in God's eyes just as surely as murder will. According to Jesus, adultery can take place not only in bed but also in our heart (Matthew 5:21-22,27-28).

9. As you think about the preceding paragraph, what are your honest reactions to it? Do God's standards seem reasonable, or unreasonable? Fair, or unjust? Achievable, or impossible? Surprising, or expected?

Second, God measures *why* we do something—our motivation—by the biblical standard that everything be done for His glory. Drawing attention to God must be the central purpose behind all our actions. "Whatever you do, do all to the glory of God" (1 Corinthians 10:31). This is why Scripture says that to sin is to "fall short of the glory of God" (Romans 3:23). If we avoid adultery only from fear of getting

> "I cannot, by direct moral effort, give myself new motives. After the first few steps in the Christian life we realise that everything which really needs to be done in our souls can be done only by God."
>
> —C. S. Lewis

74

caught, or from not wanting to destroy our marriage, or from concern for our children, but without any concern for God's name, then that avoidance (commendable as it is!) doesn't qualify as "good" from God's perspective.

10. As you consider carefully the preceding paragraph about our motivations, what thoughts or questions come to your mind? What are the most important *whys* that prompt your obedience of God, as you honestly evaluate yourself?

Finally, God measures *how* we do something by the biblical standard that everything be done in active and continual dependence on Christ ("abiding" in Him). For any of our deeds to qualify as "good" in God's eyes, He Himself must do it through us! This is why Jesus told us, "Without Me you can do nothing" (John 15:5). We can be sincerely motivated to abstain from adultery for the sake of God's glory…but how do we accomplish it? Is it simply by gritting our teeth and walking away from temptation through sheer willpower? Or is there an underlying desperation that says, "Lord, apart from Your strength and indwelling purity I will surely fall; O God, please help me appropriate Your overcoming grace to walk away"?

11. In regard to the preceding paragraph about our dependence on the Lord, what thoughts or questions come to your mind? Would you say it's hard or easy to measure up to God's standard in this area?

12. To the best of your current understanding, how would you summarize *in your own words* God's essential standards for...

(a) *what* He wants us to do?

(b) *why* we should do those things?

(c) *how* we're to do it?

Meeting God's standards on all three of these levels has been accomplished in history only by one life, and it isn't yours or mine. Only Jesus Christ always did all of the will of God, for the glory of God, through the power of God. Only the Lamb is worthy. This is why we need Him so desperately at every turn.

SPINACH IN OUR TEETH

One of the most ratlike tendencies in all of us is judging one another. Yet judging is like throwing a boomerang. Paul said, "In whatever you judge another you condemn yourself; for you who judge practice the same things" (Romans 2:1).

One evening my wife and I were washing dishes together when I noticed a fairly sizable piece of spinach caught in Sandy's teeth. It looked so funny I started laughing and somewhat gleefully pointed it out to her.

She looked at me and said, "You might want to check your own teeth."

Sure enough, my teeth sported a piece of spinach at least as big as the one in hers.

Spiritually speaking, we all have spinach in our teeth. From God's viewpoint, whenever we judge a sin in someone else's life, there's sure to be a similar kind of sin in ours if we look hard enough. We may not steal money like the thief we condemn, but *how often in a typical day do we steal the glory that belongs only to God, or steal from someone's good name by talking behind her back?*

It's easy to condemn those who are enslaved to alcohol or drugs. Normally their addiction has come about through peer pressure or seeking to escape reality. But *how often do we join with the crowd or try to numb reality through addiction to sports, shopping, overeating, or whatever?*

It seems to me that we fall into judgmentalism especially in the case of homosexuality. At its core, this sin is simply taking a legitimate longing (for love, acceptance, intimacy) and going in an illegitimate direction. *How often do we do this?* It can happen through illicit heterosexual activity or through what's often called codependency—relying on someone for what only God can provide—or through a variety of more socially acceptable means.

13. How do you find yourself responding to the questions posed in the preceding three paragraphs?

GOD'S GOOD INTENT, AND HIS GOOD REMEDY

By honestly recognizing the standards an infinitely holy God must use, we can more readily agree that there's no one among us who's righteous, no one who does good—"no, not one."

A rat is a rat is a rat.

This is dismal news. But *God's intent in clearly exposing our sinfulness is not to make us feel bad.* It's to make us feel *desperate*—to shatter every vestige of confidence in ourselves. If we merely feel disheartened or discouraged by this week's lesson, our pride still remains intact at some level. Only after we lose all hope of attaining on our own what God requires will we stop relying on self and start passionately taking hold of what God has provided.

14. How fully do you agree with the sweeping statement made at the end of the previous paragraph? Explain your thinking here.

DRUGS & SUNDAY SCHOOL

How easily and consistently we underrate our own sinful reality!

"The human heart," John Calvin observed, "has so many recesses for vanity, so many lurking places for falsehood, is so shrouded by fraud and hypocrisy, that it often deceives itself."

Even our service for God is not exempt from the flesh's control. We might teach a Sunday-school class because of sensing a genuine call from God and joyfully responding in obedience. Or it might be no more than yielding feebly to someone's pressured phone call or our fear of looking bad if we don't volunteer.

Until we understand that the passion of the flesh that drives one person to take drugs may be the same passion that drives another to teach Sunday school, we haven't yet understood the Bible's teaching on sin.

God's remedy to this deep trouble caused by our fallen nature is not an exhortation to try harder. Nor is it a program to help improve or upgrade our natural heart, since such progress is actually impossible.

No, God's solution is to offset our old heart with a new one—the "circumcised" heart He promised Israel at the border of the Promised Land. "I will give them a heart to know Me," God says (Jeremiah 24:7); "I will give you a new heart and put a new spirit within you" (Ezekiel 36:26).

We'll discover that this new heart is exactly the opposite of the old. Rather than being cold and unyielding to God, inclined toward evil, and captivated by foolishness, this one is warmly animated toward God, inclined toward righteousness, and captivated by truth.

And it's wholly the gift of God; it can only be received, not developed.

In bestowing this gift at our conversion, God doesn't remove our old heart. When we trust Christ for salvation, our sinful nature is not removed but offset. Till the day we die there will always be a godless, proud, innately wicked part of us that will never be improved over time. Yet within every believer there will also be a godly, righteous, Christ-adoring inclination that can never be destroyed (although it can be stifled by other passions).

Which nature are we depending on?

Sometimes, by listening carefully to our thoughts, we'll recognize our lingering confidence in the flesh: *I guarantee things will be different from now on... I can't believe I did something that bad; it will never happen again... If only I had tried harder.*

"When the law constrains a man to acknowledge his own corruption, and to confess his sins from the bottom of his heart, then...its task is accomplished and ended; now is the time of grace, that the blessed seed may come to raise up and comfort him who is so cast down and humbled by the law."

—Martin Luther

But with a New Covenant approach we'll learn to face reality:

"My only hope for doing better from now on is to fall back on God's strength at every turn. Please, Lord, help me do this."

"I'm frankly not too surprised I did that; when I'm not consciously depending on Christ's strength, I'm capable of doing far worse."

"No matter how hard I tried, it wouldn't have helped; I just wasn't really relying on the Lord at that moment."

15. As we prepare in the coming lessons to dive into discovering and appropriating God's New Covenant provisions, what evidence (if any) do you see in your own heart and life of lingering confidence in the flesh?

OPTIONAL FURTHER STUDY (FOR GOING IN-DEPTH)—OUR NEED FOR THE NEW COVENANT

1. *What further evidence do you see in any of the following passages of God's standards in judging us? Summarize your findings.*

   Exodus 20:1-17; Deuteronomy 27:26; Psalms 15:1-5; 24:3-4; Matthew 5:19-20; 25:31-46; Romans 14:17-18; Galatians 5:6; Hebrews 4:12-13; James 2:8-11

2. *Analyze some of the following passages to gain a clearer view of God's assess-ment of mankind's moral and spiritual condition. Summarize your findings in the space provided.*

    Matthew 12:33-37; Mark 7:14-23; Romans 3:9-12; James 1:13-15; 3:6-10; 4:1-3

3. *How would you summarize the confession Isaiah makes on behalf of God's people in Isaiah 64:6-7? And what do his words demonstrate about his insight into human character?*

Releasing Your New Purity

We must take refuge from God in God.

A. W. TOZER

The Christian life isn't hard; it's flat impossible. It becomes possible only when God injects His fullness into His people's hearts—which is exactly what He's done in the New Covenant.

With this lesson we begin exploring the New Covenant's four primary spiritual provisions: your new *purity,* your new *identity,* your new *disposition,* and your new *power.* Each is purely the gift of God alone, received through Christ alone, by faith alone. Therefore Christ alone is our key to Christian living.

Allow me to convey again what I've stressed earlier: God has *already* placed all of these provisions within you. Each one is a supernatural resource permanently residing within your soul, ready for release every day of your life on earth.

BE PARDONED OR HANG?

In 1829 a man named George Wilson was arrested for robbery and murder in a heist of the U.S. mail. He was tried, convicted, and sentenced to death by hanging.

Some friends intervened on his behalf and were finally able to obtain his pardon from President Andrew Jackson. But when Wilson was informed of his pardon, he refused it, saying he wanted to die.

This left the sheriff with quite a dilemma. How could he execute a man who was officially pardoned?

An appeal was made to President Jackson as to what to do. The perplexed president turned the matter over to the U.S. Supreme Court. Chief Justice John Marshall gave this ruling: A pardon is a piece of paper, the value of which depends on its acceptance by the person implicated. Anyone under the sentence of death would hardly be expected to refuse a pardon, but if it is refused, it's no pardon.

Thus George Wilson was executed on the gallows while his signed pardon lay a few hundred feet away on the sheriff's desk!

In the same way, God has offered His gift of divine purity to every person, a gift that not only provides pardon from eternal condemnation but offers much, much more as well. However, this unspeakably marvelous gift must be personally appropriated to be personally beneficial.

1. How does God depict our new purity in the key New Covenant passage of Ezekiel 36:25?

The divine cleansing that God promises in the New Covenant—a new purity for which only God can receive credit—is the starting point for living out our Christianity. It's what the New Testament calls being "justified" (Romans 5:1), and without it, sanctification (living the Christian life) cannot occur.

So just what does this new purity mean for us? Why is it so important? These two questions are the focal point of this lesson.

WRONG GOD?

The absolute starting point for appreciating our desperate need for this new purity is seeing God aright. This means coming to Him *as He is* and not as we have assumed Him to be or heard Him to be.

2. Imagine you're talking to someone who admits knowing nothing about God, who asks you, "What's the first thing I need to know about this God you believe in?" How would you answer?

Perhaps you might tell this seeking person that God is "a loving Father" or "your best Friend" or "an infinitely wise and powerful Being." I think it's fair to say that in our day most would go with the image of a loving Father. We expect God to warmly extend His hand down from heaven and say something like, "Hello, My name is God. I want you to know I love you and have an abundant life waiting for you." While this is blessedly true, it's no one's first brush with God.

If we follow the pattern of Paul's reasoning in the book of Romans—his most carefully sequenced letter and the New Testament's most comprehensive statement of the gospel—our starting point will be quite different. In the opening chapters of Romans, Paul's overwhelmingly predominant portrait of God is that of a holy and righteous Judge. Astonishingly, *wrath* is the first attribute of God we encounter.

3. Look for yourself at the portrait of God given in the early chapters of Romans—for example, in 1:18; 2:2-5; 3:5-6,19. Does this seem surprising at all to you? If so, why do you think this is?

Several years ago my family attended a social event in our church's gymnasium. As we entered, my youngest son, who was about four, was holding on to my pants leg. By the time we crossed the crowded gym floor, he'd somehow taken hold of another man's pants leg without realizing it. I watched for a moment as my son stood there looking around, clutching confidently. Soon I went closer, got down on one knee, looked him in the eyes, and asked how he was doing. He stared back with great surprise, shot a glance upward to see who he was holding on to, then quickly let go and ran to me. Whoops, wrong dad!

Many people, both believers and unbelievers, are confidently gripping an image of God that simply doesn't square with the God of the Bible. One of the most common of these images is that of a God who's only love and kindness, a kind of deified Mister Rogers.

OFF THE CHART

God is love, but that isn't all God is or all He's capable of. It's a shock for many believers to discover that His most foundational attribute is not love but holiness—the perfect holiness that is the source of His righteous wrath. God's holiness is His "wholly otherness," His "off the chartness." In measuring perfection on a scale of

GOD OR GRANDFATHER?

C. S. Lewis said it well:

"We want, in fact, not so much a Father in Heaven as a grandfather in Heaven—a senile old gentleman who, as they say, 'liked to see young people enjoying themselves,' and whose plan for the universe was simply that it might be truly said at the end of each day, 'A good time was had by all.'"

one to ten, God's score is always too astronomical to record. All His other attributes are shot through with this one.

Because of that holiness, one thing is sure: Nobody, but nobody, hugs God when they first encounter Him. We see it throughout Scripture: They quake in His presence; they fall at His feet, face in the dust. The experience shatters them. (See Isaiah 6:1-5; Ezekiel 1:26-28; Daniel 10:4-9; Revelation 1:12-17.)

John White speaks of "The God of White-Hot Rage" and wonders if the term sounds extreme.

> Perhaps. But you see, I'm not interested in the kind of God we want to believe in, but the God who really is.
>
> We Christians are idolaters.... We may not carve him [God] out of wood, but we do try to forget the uncomfortable parts of him and shape him to our own personal comfort.
>
> I once read an article by a man who called himself an evangelical yet talked about "the kind of God I would feel comfortable with." He at least was being honest about doing what we all do—making God into a sort of holy Teddy Bear....

OVERPOWERED AND SHATTERED

"Do you not know," Martin Luther wrote, "that God dwells in light inaccessible? We weak and ignorant creatures want to probe and understand the incomprehensible majesty of the unfathomable light of the wonder of God. We approach; we prepare ourselves to approach. What wonder then that his majesty overpowers us and shatters!"

Overpowering, shattering—that's exactly who God is. And He remains exactly that, whether or not He's given the go-ahead by you or me.

We are not called to be God's public-relations experts but to be witnesses. The only image we must project is the correct one. We aren't to aim for effect. God's character is not a subject for a media campaign designed to present His best face.

Today our natural propensity isn't so much to carve an idol from wood, but to delete from the true God those attributes we find most uncomfortable or unsettling. We're like children going unattended through a buffet line, piling on our plates only what looks most enjoyable.

"Left to ourselves," A. W. Tozer wrote, "we tend immediately to reduce God to manageable terms. We want to get Him where we can use Him, or at least know where he is when we need Him. We want a God we can in some measure control."

The love that provides us with our new purity will never astonish us unless it's seen against the backdrop of God's raging fury toward sin. When He's viewed almost exclusively as a God of love, we see forgiveness as just part of His job. That leaves His love with no punch for us, no fizz, no sparkle. *Assumed grace can never be transforming grace.* We must be primed by the blazing holiness of God before His love and forgiveness will be genuinely life changing.

Are we willing to risk coming to God as He is and not as we would like Him to be? This is no easy step, but if we do, our lives will never be the same.

4. How would you answer the question in the preceding paragraph as it relates to you? To answer yes, what would this mean for you in practical, everyday terms?

Lion Attack

Imagine for a moment we're at a zoo. As we look together at the animals, you reach down over a fence and pet the head of a small lamb. The lamb lifts its head and licks your hand. "That's nice," you think, before we stroll on to see more.

Suddenly you hear me screaming, "Look out!" You turn. Approaching you is the largest, fiercest lion you've ever seen. He's just escaped his cage, and you're his lunch if he so chooses.

There's no escape. He's rushing toward you, his jaws opening ever wider—he's upon you! And he licks your hand, then stands peacefully at your side. You breathe an incredibly deep sigh.

Which lick would mean more to you—that of the lion or that of the lamb? Obviously, the lion's. Why? Because he could just as easily crush you in his jaws, an option the lamb doesn't have.

The primary reason people aren't astonished and exuberant over the Lamb's forgiveness is that they have little or no sense of the Lion's raging fury against their sins. Until we've trembled on death row, we won't dance at the granting of our pardon.

In John's vision in Revelation it is only after he beholds "the Lion of the tribe of Judah" that he sees "a Lamb as though it had been slain" (Revelation 5:5-6). The order is inviolable. Our Lord will never be appreciated as the Lamb unless He's first encountered as the Lion.

How wonderful, how beautiful, the sight of Thee must be,

Thine endless wisdom, boundless power, and awful purity.

O how I fear Thee, living God, with deepest, tenderest fears,

And worship Thee with trembling hope, and penitential tears.

—F. W. Faber

HELL

It's because of the Lion's perfect wrath that there's such a place as hell where sinners spend an eternity in torment, although no doctrine is more abhorrent to modern man.

This peril faced by all unbelievers is an *awful* one. The primary image in Scripture is that of everlasting fire, a fire that "is not quenched" (Mark 9:43-48). Whether the fire is literal or figurative is really not important. Whatever the punishment is, it's to the soul of man what fire is to his flesh, only more so. No words can possibly describe what it is to face the unrestrained fury of the perfect wrath of the infinite, almighty God.

This state is also *unalterable.* There's no second chance once an unbeliever has passed into eternity. In Luke 16:19-31, Jesus told how Abraham (with the beggar Lazarus beside him in paradise) answered the miserable cries from Hades of the man who once was rich: "Between us and you," Abraham called, "there is a great

IN AN ANGRY GOD'S HANDS

Jonathan Edwards is probably best known for his sermon titled "Sinners in the Hands of an Angry God." Why did he preach this message on God's everlasting wrath?

I agree wholeheartedly with R. C. Sproul's analysis:

"He did this not out of a sadistic delight in frightening people, but out of compassion. He loved his congregation enough to warn them of the dreadful consequences of facing the wrath of God. He was not concerned with laying a guilt trip on his people but with awakening them to the peril they faced if they remained unconverted."

gulf fixed, so that those who want to pass from here to you cannot, nor can those from there pass to us." It has been well noted that the rich man at that point became an ardent supporter of missions; he begged Abraham to send Lazarus to testify to the man's five brothers "lest they also come to this place of torment." Hell was so awful he wanted no one he loved to join him there.

This experience of God's wrath will also be *eternal.* It is "everlasting destruction" (2 Thessalonians 1:9). Unbelievers have no hope of simply being annihilated, consumed out of existence; instead, Jesus described hell as the place where "their worm does not die" (Mark 9:48).

Jonathan Edwards gave sinners this warning:

> It would be dreadful to suffer this fierceness and wrath of Almighty God one moment; but you must suffer it for all eternity. There will be no end to this exquisite horrible misery. When you look forward, you shall see a long forever, a boundless duration before you, which will swallow up your thoughts, and amaze your soul; and you will absolutely despair of ever having any deliverance, any end, any mitigation, any rest at all. You will know certainly that you must wear out long ages, millions of millions of ages, in wrestling and conflicting with this almighty merciless vengeance: and then when you have so done, when so many ages have actually been spent by you in this manner…you will know that all is but a point to what remains…. Your punishment will indeed be infinite.

All this is why we commit an unspeakably grave offense toward unbelievers when we highlight for them only the love of God and fail to warn them with tears of the horrors lying ahead if they remain unconverted.

5. How do you respond to the points made in this section about hell? Do you fully accept and believe them? Do they raise any doubts or questions in your mind? Record your thoughts here:

OUR STARTING POINT FOR PURITY

In light of what we've explored of God's wrath and holiness, let's ask the question again: What does God's gift of our wonderful new purity mean for us?

6. Look again at those key New Covenant promises in Jeremiah 31:31-34. At the very end of this passage, what does God promise to do in regard to His people's sin?

7. In Isaiah 43:25, what specific *purpose* does God give for doing this?

8. How thoroughly and completely does God promise to do this, according to Jeremiah 50:20, Psalm 103:10-12, and Colossians 2:12-14?

The starting point for our new purity is the forgiveness of our sins. When God promises in the New Covenant to "remember no more" our sins, it's a figure of speech. Obviously an omniscient God cannot actually forget anything, but He can choose to send our sins away and never, ever hold them against us. The justly deserved penalty for our sins is permanently canceled—not because the charges were dropped, but because they've been paid in full by Someone else.

This forgiveness means that we can look forward with absolute assurance to an endless future spent in that place where "there shall be no more death, nor sorrow, nor crying. There shall be no more pain, for the former things have passed away" (Revelation 21:4). Jonathan Edwards might just as easily have said, "It would be wonderful to enjoy this grace and kindness of Almighty God one moment; but you will enjoy it for all eternity. There will be no end to this exquisite joy. When you look forward, you'll see a long forever, a boundless duration before you, which will swallow up your thoughts and amaze your souls; and you'll absolutely rejoice in not having any end or mitigation of this at all."

Christianity is the only religion that guarantees heaven and its unending enjoyment up front. Every believer is guaranteed eternity in heaven—*no matter what happens after we trust Christ for salvation.*

But does the Bible really teach such a risky truth?

CATASTROPHICALLY GOOD

The experience of eternity in God's presence will be so overwhelmingly wonderful that J. R. R. Tolkien coined a great word for it—"eucatastrophe." Heaven will be catastrophically good, and catastrophically good *forever.*

Every believer is guaranteed this catastrophic goodness—no matter what happens after trusting Christ for salvation.

SAFE IN HIS GRIP

Jesus said this about His followers: "I give them eternal life, and *they shall never perish;* neither shall anyone snatch them out of My hand." We're safe in His grip. Then Jesus added, "My Father, who has given them to Me, is greater than all; and no one is able to snatch them out of My Father's hand" (John 10:28-29). We're in the Father's grip as well!

Is it even theoretically possible to be more eternally secure than to rest in the grip of the Father and the Son at the same time? No wonder Christ says we "shall never perish"!

SAVED IN THE PAST, SAVED NOW, SAVED IN THE FUTURE

In a statement from Jesus in John 5:24, we're given three time frames regarding the absolute certainty of our salvation. Once we've trusted Christ, three things are immediately and unalterably true.

The first time frame is the present: "Most assuredly," Jesus says, "he who hears My word and believes in Him who sent Me *has everlasting life.*" We have it now. Already it's ours.

The next time frame concerns the future: "Most assuredly," Jesus says, "he who hears My word and believes...*shall not* [literally, "shall in no possible way"] *come into judgment.*" While every believer will stand before the judgment seat of Christ for reward within heaven, none will ever stand before God to be judged in regards to entrance into heaven.

The third time frame regards our past: "Most assuredly," Jesus says, "he who hears My word and believes...*has passed from death into life.*"

WHO CAN REALLY KNOW FOR SURE?

Some will say that it's presumptive and arrogant to claim to know that we're saved. Such language *would* be arrogant if we ourselves had anything whatsoever to do with securing our salvation. But there's zero room for our boasting, except in what a great God we have. Our salvation is wholly "the *gift* of God, not of works, lest anyone should boast" (Ephesians 2:8-9).

"God has *given* us eternal life," John reminds us, "and this life is in His Son." Our possession of eternal life centers on one issue alone—having Christ in our lives. "He who has the Son has life," John continues; "he who does not have the Son of God does not have life." The *only* requirement for knowing that we have eternal life is that we have God's Son in our life through simple faith. Then John adds another clincher: "These things I have written to you who believe in the name of the Son of God, that you may *know* that you have eternal life" (1 John 5:11-13). Not "that you may hope," not "that you may guess," not "that you may be fairly sure." He says, "that you may *know.*"

9. Think clearly and honestly about this question: Are you certain of your eternal salvation? If not, what keeps you from being certain?

YOU'RE DISCOVERED!

10. Look at Hebrews 9:14, as well as the follow-up statement in Hebrews 10:22. What does Christ's blood do for us? And how does this differ from forgiveness?

Besides forgiveness and the assurance of eternal life, our new purity also means we're *cleansed* from those sins. While forgiveness takes care of sin's *penalty*, cleansing takes care of sin's *guilt*. Through forgiveness we escape the torments of hell; through cleansing we escape the torments of conscience.

According to a commonly told story, Sir Arthur Conan Doyle, author of the Sherlock Holmes series, once decided to play a practical joke on twelve of his friends. To each he sent an anonymous telegram that simply read, "Flee at once…all is discovered." Within twenty-four hours, all twelve had fled the country!

All of us, in varying degrees, know what it is to live with such guilt nagging at our consciences, depleting our souls of any real joy. Our flesh has several ways of trying to deal with that guilt. Perhaps the most common is to shift the blame in another direction. Or we try to hide the sins that cause our guilt, perhaps by giving them a softer label: "codependency," "midlife crisis," "personality weakness." We may attempt to bury our guilt through immersion in life's busyness. Or we try making up for our sin through penance—self-punishment.

None of these responses, however, can bring the deep joy of a genuinely cleansed conscience. Only Christ's blood will "cleanse your conscience from dead works" (Hebrews 9:14). There's no other path to peace within—but it's all ours in our new purity.

OUR ALIEN CLOTHING

11. Look up 2 Corinthians 5:21. Because of what Christ has done for us, what do we become? What does this mean, and why is it important?

With God's gift of purity, not only is something infinitely negative—sin's penalty and our guilt before God—now taken away, but something infinitely positive is added: We're permanently *clothed* in bestowed righteousness. With all God's people we can declare, "He has clothed me with the garments of salvation, He has covered me with the robe of righteousness" (Isaiah 61:10). It's like not only washing your car, but waxing it as well. Not only are we clean from the dirt of sin; we're also completely and eternally "coated" with the perfect righteousness of Christ.

Luther called this an "alien" or "foreign" righteousness. It's a righteousness wholly belonging to God and wholly bestowed by God, utterly alien to our natural, corrupt state but completely native to God's perfect holiness. And now it's *ours!*

As believers we're more than forgiven sinners; we're saints decked out in the finest wardrobe heaven has to offer. At every moment, in every situation, we're wholly enveloped in God-wrought purity that ensures our Father's unconditional and complete acceptance.

This new purity brings a humble, grateful dignity to the child of God. The dignity comes from the fact that we're now worthy to come boldly before God's throne at all times; the humility comes from the fact that *we* had absolutely nothing to do with this worthiness.

12. Are you absolutely convinced of your cleansing and of your being clothed in the righteousness of Christ? Are those truths residing within you at heart level or only at an intellectual level? Record your thoughts here:

ASSURANCE EVERY MOMENT

So we have it: Our *forgiveness* lets us know we can be *vigorously* assured (we'll talk more about that) of our eternal destiny. We need never fear that some sin might move us out of range from God's grace. As Paul assures us, "Where sin abounded, grace abounded much more" (Romans 5:20). Forgiveness provides the security of our perfect eternal destiny. At any moment when I may doubt I'm really saved, this truth reminds me that assurance is found by focusing upon Christ's cross.

Our *cleansing* lets us know that the Enemy's accusations are forever silenced. At all times we are those who have "hearts sprinkled from an evil conscience and our bodies washed with pure water" (Hebrews 10:22). At any moment when I feel overwhelmed by guilt, this truth reminds me that I *always* approach God not on the basis of my performance, but solely on the basis of His Son's blood, which has cleansed me from all sin.

And being *clothed* in Christ's righteousness lets us know that we can come boldly before God and His throne of grace. Being robed in the righteousness of Christ provides the humble dignity of God-given significance. At any moment when what seems most real to me is my personal failure, this truth reminds me that my value isn't found primarily in who I am, but in who and what envelops me.

STRUCK BY LIGHTNING

Recently my son and I were driving in a thunderstorm when our car was struck by lightning. Immediately the car's horn blared uncontrollably, the lights on the

TOTAL CLEANSING

A story is told that one night the devil approached Martin Luther with a long list of the reformer's sins—lust, greed, and more.

Luther, however, pointed out that the list wasn't long enough and proceeded to mention other transgressions the devil should record as well. The list finally completed, Luther told Satan, "Now write at the bottom these words"—and he quoted 1 John 1:7: "The blood of Jesus Christ His Son cleanses us from *all* sin."

At that, the devil fled instantly.

dashboard blinked crazily, the car no longer accelerated, and we smelled smoke from all the wires that had just been fried. And yet, although we saw the flash and heard the rifling crack of thunder, we never *felt* a thing. Inside that car, we were safe.

The wrath of God is far more real and powerful and destructive than that lightning. But on the cross, Jesus took in His own body the full fury of the bolt of that wrath, wrath that *we* had earned. We who are "in Christ" are utterly safe from any possibility of God's wrath striking us. In Christ we'll never feel a thing of all that He had to bear to perfectly preserve us from the fiery assault of God's wrath. "Jesus paid it all, all to Him I owe."

What a wonder, then, is the gift of God's purity!

THE EXPRESSION ON GOD'S FACE

13. Fix in your mind the image of God looking down at you day by day. Then honestly answer this question: How would you describe His facial expression toward you? Is He joyful? Sad? Disappointed? Upset? Is He smiling, frowning, yawning, or just expressionless? (Don't worry about being theologically correct; just be honest.) Record your answer here:

Asking that of myself, I find often that my heart hasn't caught up with what my mind knows to be doctrinally true. When I think of all the failures and missed opportunities in my life, it's hard to imagine God looking down with anything but disappointment written all over His face. That's why the truths in this lesson are so important to me. Time and again I've retreated to them to regain my footing on how God truly sees me.

I believe that many, many Christians feel they're living under God's frown. They can easily relate to the following candid account from a struggling missionary.

God's demands of me were so high, and His opinion of me was so low, there was no way for me to live except under His frown.… All day long He nagged me: "Why don't you pray more? Why don't you witness more? When will you ever learn self-discipline? How can you allow yourself to indulge in such wicked thoughts? Do this. Don't do that. Yield, confess, work harder." God was always using His love against me. He'd show me His nail-pierced hands, and then He would look at me glaringly and say, "Well, why aren't you a better Christian? Get busy and live the way you ought to."

Most of all, I had a God who down underneath considered me to be less than dirt. Oh, He made a great ado about loving me, but I believed that the day-to-day love and acceptance I longed for could only be mine if I let Him crush everything that was really me. When I came down to it, there was scarcely a word or a feeling or a thought or a decision of mine that God really liked.

These words were written before this person had a life-changing encounter with God's grace and a fresh appreciation of her new purity in Him. But I appreciate her brutal honesty in articulating what many of us have felt in varying degrees.

14. Can you identify with the struggling missionary's words? How does her account reflect your own thoughts and experiences, past or present?

What does Scripture say about God's expression as He views us? At the risk of sounding irreverent, let me put it this way: *He's smiling from ear to ear!* His fundamental disposition toward you and toward me is that of passionate, loving pursuit and exuberant, unbridled joy. This doesn't mean He isn't displeased over our sinful actions or attitudes. But toward our *person* He is incessantly moving forward in gladsome love.

God's Word makes this promise: "He will rejoice over you with gladness, He will quiet you in His love, He will rejoice over you with singing" (Zephaniah 3:17). Let those words sink deep into your soul—God is singing joyously over you!

Why is this true? *Because when God looks at you, He sees Jesus first.* "Your life," after all, "is *hidden* with Christ in God" (Colossians 3:3). And God cannot look upon His Son without a smile creasing His face and explosive joy rising in His heart. "This is My beloved Son, in whom I am well pleased" (Matthew 3:17), He fairly shouted two thousand years ago. This is what happens today when God looks upon you, because of your permanent submergence in His Son.

Pause now and try to visualize God smiling broadly as He looks down upon you. Now say to yourself seven times, "God is singing over me with joy!" (If you end up shouting it, that's okay.) The Person who matters most, the Father you'll spend eternity with, the God of unrivaled power—His eyes are now dancing around you with sheer delight as He sings over you, smiling from ear to ear. He

THE LAMB WHO HIDES US

In the Chinese language, the word for "righteousness" is the combination of two pictures. On top is the figure of a lamb; directly beneath is that of a person.

What a perfect image of the righteousness that Christ alone provides! Whenever the Father looks down at you, He first sees the perfect Lamb of God, "hiding" you.

Certainly God is aware of any sin in our lives, but that isn't what He's *primarily* aware of in any believer. What He sees first and foremost is the beauty of His Son enveloping us.

cannot do otherwise, for you're united with His Son. You are "accepted [literally, "highly favored"] in the Beloved" (Ephesians 1:6).

15. Think again of how you earlier envisioned the expression on God's face as He watches you on a typical day. From what you've seen in this lesson, is this image a correct one? Why or why not?

OPTIONAL FURTHER STUDY (FOR GOING IN-DEPTH)—FORGIVENESS AND HOLINESS

1. *Read Hebrews 10:1-14, a passage that contrasts Christ's sacrifice with the Old Testament sacrificial system. Explore these contrasts by answering the following questions:*

   (a) Under the Old Covenant, whose blood covered sins?

   (b) Whose blood covers sins in the New Covenant?

   (c) How often were the blood sacrifices made under the Old Covenant?

(d) How often are the blood sacrifices made in the New Covenant?

(e) What were the Old Covenant sacrifices unable to do?

(f) How does this change under the New Covenant?

2. *How should a deep and intense understanding of our cleansing through Christ's blood affect us? How should it affect the way we view God, ourselves, and others? Look up some of the following passages to find those that speak most directly to you on this subject. If the verses are familiar, revisit them in the*

ONE LAMB

Scholars estimate that from the time of Moses to the time of Christ, some two million lambs had been slaughtered on God's altar for the yearly atonement sacrifices.

But Christ was not *a* lamb but *the* Lamb—"Behold! The Lamb of God who takes away the sin of the world!" (John 1:29). He was the once and final Lamb destined for sacrifice, the One whom all others merely foreshadowed.

fresh light of what you've learned so far in this workbook. Let the awesome power of these truths come alive for you. Then record how these passages encourage and strengthen you.

Isaiah 53:7-11; 1 Corinthians 6:9-11; Colossians 2:11-14; Hebrews 9:11-15; 10:19-22

3. *Now consider how our cleansing and forgiveness are related both to God's holiness and to ours. Let the passages listed here stimulate your meditation on this. Find the verses that speak most to you, and write down your reflections.*

Exodus 15:11-13; Leviticus 20:7-8,26; Psalm 99:8-9; Isaiah 62:11-12; 1 Corinthians 1:30-31; Ephesians 5:1-2; 2 Timothy 1:8-10; 1 Peter 1:16-19

"It is only when we are delivered from the guilt of sin that we can understand or exhibit the true power of holiness."

—C. H. Mackintosh

Dangerous—and Worth the Risk

Then suddenly there dawns upon us the vast, entire endowment
of God's free love and forgiveness.... It is this which bowls
us over...frees us...transforms us.

PAUL TOURNIER

Our New Covenant gift of purity springs from something dangerous, something worth a fresh look—God's grace.

Years ago my family first visited the Grand Canyon. It was a beautiful, clear day, and the sheer majesty of the sight before me took my breath away. So did the shortage of guardrails. Our young boys naturally wanted to race to the very edge and look over. My instinct was to hold them back, safe from any danger of falling. I was only too glad to describe the beauty to them if they would stay back ten yards or so. Somehow they didn't like that idea. After all, to get the total impact, to fully appreciate the canyon's awesome beauty, you must go right to the edge.

Grace is like that. If it's to take our breath away and significantly possess our lives, we must go right to the edge—where the overwhelming astonishment of grace and the potential abuse of grace linger side by side.

All too often the church has erected safeguards and restrictions to keep people back from the danger of abusing grace and falling into license and lawlessness. In doing so we create an even greater danger—keeping people's view of grace so distant that they fail to have a breathtaking appreciation for the real thing.

In this lesson we'll see more clearly how amazing God's grace really is—not just in how He redeemed us, but even more in the quality of day-to-day living that He both invites us to and fully outfits us for. We'll seek to bring into sharper awareness the undiluted, unrestricted flow of His grace into our daily lives. As we do so, we'll discover the delightfully unexpected result in what it does for our purity and godly living.

GOD'S SAFETY NET

During the initial stages of constructing the famous Golden Gate Bridge, twenty-three workers fell to their deaths in the cold waters connecting the North Pacific to San Francisco Bay. Finally, halfway through the project, a large net was put in place beneath the bridge. Surprisingly, from then on only ten men actually fell—all safely caught by the net. Beyond this, there was a full 25 percent increase in the workers' productivity rate. Assured that their safety was no longer in question, they pursued their work with far greater freedom and effectiveness than before.

This is exactly what God has done for us. Stretched wide beneath us, extending from eternity past to eternity future, is God's perfect grace, assuring every believer that we can never fall from His favor. No matter how badly we falter or fail, we can never plunge past the grace of God.

IRRATIONAL, UNIMAGINABLE, POWERFUL

If grace makes sense to you, I doubt you're close enough to really see it. The real thing defies comprehension...but not experience. Grace is God's irrational, unimaginable kindness. Yet the word is used so often among believers that we've become callous to its intended impact.

1. (a) What does the biblical word *grace* mean to you? How would you describe or picture it in a way that captures its true impact upon you?

   (b) How would you explain the difference between grace and mercy, as you understand those two terms?

In the New Covenant, God's grace goes beyond anything offered by the world's religions. Virtually all faiths have justice as a primary tenet: Man gets what he deserves (as is particularly true in Islam and Hinduism). Many religions also add the concept of mercy, which is man *not* getting all the punishment he deserves. Christianity alone introduces the full concept of grace—of getting, with no good reason, what we positively *don't* deserve. Grace goes miles beyond mercy.

Grace is the most unreasonable thing in the world. It's also the most powerful. Nothing is more effective for transforming lives, risky though it is.

I well remember my first encounter with grace. I was five years old and our family was on vacation in California. One day at lunch I flatly refused to eat my soup, so my mother said I could have nothing else to eat before dinner.

Late in the afternoon my father and I were running errands together. We stopped in a drugstore where he ordered an ice cream cone, then turned and asked if I'd like one as well. I reminded him of Mom's injunction at lunchtime. With a smile I can still remember, he said he knew what she'd said, but I could still have an ice cream cone if I wanted. Gladly I placed my order.

I don't endorse what my father did as particularly good parenting, but it was my first marvelous experience of clearly getting something I didn't deserve.

One year later my father died of cancer. Today, I can't recall even one spanking he gave me (my mother has assured me there were many), but that event in a California drugstore stays in my memory as my most vivid recollection of him. Burned most deeply into a young boy's psyche was not his father's justice but the precious commodity of grace.

Nothing captures and transforms a person's soul like the power of true grace.

UNRESTRAINED EXUBERANCE

One of the greatest portraits of grace is the father's response to his prodigal son in the story Jesus told in Luke 15.

2. Read through this familiar parable once more (in Luke 15:11-32), and this time jot down your impressions of how the father demonstrated grace in his response to his son.

We read in this story that while the son "was still a great way off, his father saw him." We sense that amid his daily work the father had been continually scanning the horizon. Likewise, God's grace isn't something *we* must search for, but something *He* is on the lookout to offer.

GRACE'S POWER

One Saturday morning years ago, I decided to surprise my wife with breakfast in bed. I hurried to a nearby McDonald's and ordered at the drive-through. When I pulled forward to the pickup window, I discovered I was about ninety cents short.

Quite embarrassed, I told the lady at the window I had miscalculated and couldn't buy the meal after all. She asked how much I had. When I told her, she smiled and said that would be enough and handed me my order. I told her I'd go home, get the ninety cents, and come right back to pay her, but she told me not to worry about it. I then promised that the next time I came to that McDonald's I would pay the difference. She laughed and told me to just go home, enjoy breakfast, and quit worrying about what I owed. I drove away, grateful for this token of grace.

The next time I drove down that street looking to grab a fast breakfast, guess where I found myself naturally wanting to go? It was McDonald's—not because I had to or wanted to make up for what I'd done, but simply because I'd received something freely that I in no way deserved and my heart was unable to remain unaffected by it.

Such is the power of genuine grace in any form.

Perhaps, as you read these words, God is convicting you of having strayed from Him. Know for sure that He hasn't given up on you; He is, in fact, craning His neck for your return.

We also see in this story the unrestrained exuberance of grace: "His father saw him and had compassion, and ran and fell on his neck and kissed him." In that culture, an older man running toward someone was considered highly undignified. But God's grace is so much more than dignified patience or enduring niceness.

3. What demonstrations do you see of God's compassion and unrestrained exuberance for His people in Hosea 11:8-9 and Zephaniah 3:17?

Have you ever pictured God running after you to hold you close and tell you how much He loves you? His grace cannot be tamed or kept in check when one of His beloved comes back to Him. Always He *feels deeply* for us. It's an unbridled passion, the kind that can ignite our own passion toward Him in response.

Consider well this father's embrace of his returning son. It wasn't an extended handshake of guarded love. No, he "ran and fell on his neck and kissed him." The Greek verb tense denotes repeated action—kissing again and again. Yet imagine how this son must have smelled—of swine, of sweat, of days on the dusty road. Repulsive? No more so than when God embraced you and me in all our sin at the cross. There we experienced His divine bear hug, lifting us off our feet, holding us close in spite of our filth.

As the prodigal approached his home, what might he reasonably have expected his father's response to be? Perhaps first of all, a curt command to get cleaned up.

Then a stiff lecture laying out the rules for his staying, probationary guidelines, a repayment plan for the squandered wealth. After all, shouldn't forgiveness be extended only when safeguards against its abuse are put in place?

Instead the son found absolutely unconditional forgiveness and acceptance, which is exactly what greets us in our every encounter with our Father.

AN UNCEASING FLOW

In Jesus' story, the grace continues in an unceasing flow. The father tells the servants, "Bring out the best robe...a ring...sandals.... And bring the fatted calf...and let us eat and be merry." Grace is unimaginable in generosity. It gives beyond all reasonable expectation.

The "best" (literally, "first") robe signified special honor. Likewise when you and I came to the foot of the cross for salvation, God not only forgave us but also clothed us with the finest robe available, the righteousness of Christ.

Rings in that day were used to press a seal into wax to validate a transaction. The father's gift of a ring signifies the granting of his authority. It was like giving the son the family credit card. (If this were *your* son, how quickly would you have handed over your American Express?) Grace is willing to take risks that human reasoning never considers.

When you and I trusted Christ, we were given immediate authority to conduct business in the Father's name. Do we deserve this outlandish privilege? Of course not. But then again, nothing in the sphere of grace comes because it's deserved.

The father also called for sandals for the feet of his son, who most likely had returned barefoot. This gift speaks of restored intimacy, for in that day only slaves or the extremely poor went without sandals. The son had come home intending to become his father's slave; before he could even say so, his father reaffirmed his sonship. Despite the rebellion, his relationship with his father had never been in question. He was a son when he left home; he was a son while feeding pigs; he was a son when he returned home; he would be a son forever. Grace alone provides the security of divine relationship that can never be lost.

THE PRODIGAL FATHER

On top of all this, the father called for a celebration, proving even further his unsparing generosity. In fact, do you know the original definition for the word *prodigal?* We usually think it means "wayward," but it comes from a root that means "excessive or overflowing." A *prodigy* is someone profusely talented; a prodigious writer is known for his vast outflow of words. The son in Jesus' story is called "prodigal" for spending extravagant wealth on extravagant pleasures. But I think this story is really the parable of *the prodigal father*—one who gives to the undeserving with outrageous generosity and irrational kindness. Such is the grace and love of God, surpassing our wildest hopes.

We see this outrageous generosity and irrational kindness of God most clearly in the cross. Here's my own very free translation of Romans 5:8—"God demonstrates His own special brand of love toward us, in that while we were in the pigpen, Christ spilled His precious blood for unworthies such as us."

Such excessive grace doesn't mean God doesn't sometimes discipline us. But His fundamental, unwavering disposition toward us, His blood-bought children, is relentless, unwavering, wholesale, lavish acceptance. We're now and forever "accepted in the Beloved" (Ephesians 1:6).

4. Choose some of the verses on the following page to look for evidence of God's "outrageous generosity and irrational kindness." If the passages are familiar, ask the Holy Spirit to help you see and experience their truth in a fresh and powerful way. Write down what you observe, and use these observations to express your worship of God.

Isaiah 49:13-23; John 13:1-5; 14:2-4; Romans 8:31-39; Ephesians 1:3; 1 John 3:1-2

THE POTENTIAL FOR ABUSE

Well now, we might think, *if that's the way of God's grace—if my every sin is more than forgiven—why not give grace a good workout? More fun for me, more glory for God (since I allow Him to demonstrate ever more grace). What a deal! Live like I want to now…then enjoy heaven as well when I die.*

That is the *flesh's* response to God's grace.

5. What did Paul say in Romans 5:20-21 that might have caused his readers to have this exact response?

The flesh response to grace is a reaction Paul anticipated and had in fact encountered. "What shall we say then?" he went on to ask rhetorically. "Shall we continue in sin that grace may abound?" Immediately he responded, "Certainly not!" (Romans 6:1-2). But what were his reasons for that conclusion?

First, notice the reasons he *didn't* give. Paul nowhere said that if you continue living in sin, you'll lose your salvation. Nor did he say that if you continue in sin, you weren't really saved in the first place.

What he *did* say in essence is this: We should no longer live how we used to live *because we're no longer who we used to be.* He exclaimed, "How shall we who died to sin live any longer in it?" (Romans 6:2).

Paul, the apostle of grace, was never accused of being a legalist, but he was accused of promoting license and irresponsible living. Here was the charge of antinomianism ("against law"—living any way you please), an accusation that is continually hurled at those who faithfully proclaim the gospel. "The true preaching of the gospel of salvation by grace alone always leads to this charge being brought against it," wrote D. Martyn Lloyd-Jones, the great British pastor and Bible teacher. He said that if you preach the genuine gospel, your accusers will say your message "really amounts to this: That because you are saved by grace alone it does not matter at all what you do; you can go on sinning as much as you like because it will redound all the more to the glory of grace.

"There is no better test as to whether a man is really preaching the New Testament gospel of salvation than this," Lloyd-Jones declared. "If my preaching and presentation of the gospel of salvation does not expose it to that misunderstanding, then it is not the gospel."

It's true, of course, that grace is sometimes abused, and such abuse is terrible and tragic. Jude spoke of the condemnation of those "who turn the grace of our God into lewdness" (Jude 4). But the cure is never to control grace through restrictions and qualifications. *If grace doesn't have the potential to be abused, it won't have the power to transform.* For grace to move powerfully in our lives it must remain unbridled and unrestricted from our well-intentioned safeguards.

For the believer, already cleansed by the blood of Christ, our sin doesn't negate our relationship with God, but it does affect our intimacy with Him. To restore this intimacy requires genuine confession of specific sins. Our new purity through

Christ's blood ensures God's everlasting acceptance, while confession of known sins ensures His present communion with our souls.

VIGOROUS ASSURANCE

In the previous lesson I used the term "vigorous assurance" in regard to knowing our eternal destiny. I choose that word *vigorous* as opposed to "tentative" or "partial" assurance. Historically the church has seemed reticent to give believers the kind of full-fledged, out-and-out assurance of salvation that the New Covenant provides. More than for any other reason, this has been done by well-intentioned saints to safeguard grace from abuse. Their desire to see purity in the church is commendable, but their safeguarding of grace also saps it of its full vitality.

6. In what ways, if any, do you think you might have been guilty at times of "overprotecting" grace in this way, either in your own life or in your view of others?

One of the ways we erect these safeguards is to teach that a believer will lose his salvation if he wanders far enough from the Lord. But if we remove the concept of eternal security, we drive a stake right through the heart of grace and drain it of its lifeblood. The absolute assurance of being heaven-bound—solely through God's grace and Christ's righteousness—is the sort of unreasonable kindness that can seize and hold your heart and life like nothing else known to man.

The love and grace that incite such kindness are astonishing beyond words.

"Behold what manner of love the Father has bestowed on us," we read in 1 John 3:1. Just exactly what "manner" of love is this? Jesus tells us it's precisely the *same* love with which the Father loves Jesus, His only begotten Son. "You have sent Me," He prayed, "and have loved them *as* You have loved Me" (John 17:23).

Such a concept—that God's love for me matches His love for Christ—seems impossible if not heretical. Yet this is what Scripture says.

How can it be true? One reason is that *perfect, eternal love is incapable of loving at varying degrees.* God loves at only one level—perfection. Another reason is that God loves us *because of who He is, not who we are.* His love for us is unchanging because God is unchanging—always faithful in His commitment toward us.

7. How do you respond to the statement that God's love for you matches His love for Jesus Christ? Can you fully accept and believe that? If not, why not? (You may want to examine closely John 17:20-26.)

8. Are you convinced that no genuine believer in Christ can ever lose his or her salvation? If not, how do you see the passages on the following page speaking to this issue? Summarize your findings in the space provided.

John 5:24; 1 Corinthians 3:10-15; Colossians 2:13-14; 1 John
5:11-13

Putting Our New Purity to Work

How do we take hold of this grace experientially? In a word, it's by *faith*.

Luther called faith "the 'yes' of the heart, a conviction on which one stakes one's
life." How do you think of faith? What synonyms come to mind?

I believe that one of the clearest verses in the Bible that describe true saving
faith is Romans 4:5. Take a moment to write out this verse here and to ponder what
it says:

Notice how this verse demonstrates a recognition of personal need, the refusal
to trust in any personal effort or religious rite, and a sole reliance on the justification that comes from God through Christ.

I believe the essence of faith is dependence, a dependence rooted in a genuine
and overwhelming sense of need. That's why the Sermon on the Mount begins,

"Blessed are the poor in spirit, for theirs is the kingdom of heaven" (Matthew 5:3). Brokenness and faith are so closely intertwined, it's difficult to tell where one ends and the other begins.

Several years ago our church's college ministry was studying Romans. Among these students was a young woman who grew up in a strong Christian home, had gone to a Christian school, and was now involved in several Christian activities on campus. She was engaged to a seminary student and was on her way to becoming a pastor's wife. About halfway into the semester she announced to her small group that she'd just become a Christian. At first they laughed, but she told them she was dead serious. While studying Romans she had realized for the first time that *she* was a sinner. She had known that Christ died for sinners, but she had never truly counted herself among that group until the Spirit of God opened her eyes to her own sinfulness. Only then did she genuinely believe.

TURNING AWAY, TURNING TOWARD

True faith also requires that we consciously empty our hands of all personal merit if we're to genuinely take hold of the cross and experience God's gift of our new purity. We don't have saving faith if we come to Christ believing that salvation is a combination of trusting Him *plus* something else baptism, living a moral life, church attendance, whatever. We must *turn away* from any wrong object of trust. This is the fundamental idea behind the word *repentance,* which literally means "to change the mind."

In true faith we also *turn to* the right object of trust—and only Christ is worthy of our trust. Only by embracing the Person of Christ can our new purity be received and known. "For Christ is the end of the law for righteousness to everyone who believes" (Romans 10:4).

Imagine you're desperately thirsty and a cup of clear, cold water is placed before you. You're definitely aware of what's there; you're also certain that it can quench your thirst. But when does it actually make a practical difference in your life? Only when you receive it—in other words, *drink.* Until then your thirst remains untouched, no matter how firmly you give mental assent to the reality and significance of that cold water in front of you. To genuinely believe is not only to agree, but also to appropriate (John 1:12; 7:37-38).

9. Perhaps there are some aspects of your Christian faith that you *believe* in the sense of "agreeing" they're true, but you haven't yet fully appropriated them into your life. Do you think this might be true? If so, what aspects of Christian life or doctrine might be involved—things that you mentally agree with but haven't yet staked your life on?

"Faith holds out the hand and the sack and just lets the good be done to it. For as God is the giver who bestows such things in His love, we are the receivers who receive the gift through faith which does nothing. For it is not our doing and cannot be merited by our work. It has already been granted and given. You need only open your mouth, or rather, your heart, and keep still, and let yourself be filled."

—Martin Luther

Saving Faith?

We must be careful to call people to exercise this true faith as we present the gospel. "Faith," wrote J. Gresham Machen, "consists not in doing something, but in receiving something."

10. Suppose you're with a friend, and the conversation takes a spiritual turn. You probe a little, and your friend says he "gave his life" to Christ at a church camp when he was fifteen, but he has never felt really sure that it "took." How would you guide the conversation from there?

A good place to start with a friend like this would be the standard diagnostic question, "Let's suppose you and I died tonight and we both went before God. If God were to ask you, 'Why should I let you into heaven?' how would you answer Him?"

When I ask that question and the person's response includes anything whatsoever about being a good person or doing good things, I immediately assume he isn't saved. I may find out later that he is a Christian and was just fuzzy in his beliefs, but most often that isn't the case.

Gospel invitations that present becoming a Christian as a matter of "giving" or "surrendering" your life to Christ often confuse the real issue. Although God clearly calls every believer to all-out surrender to Christ as Lord, this comes only *after* the person has been made a new creation in Christ and has the resources necessary for such a life. To require the unbeliever to give his all to Christ is like telling a person with no legs to get up and walk. Someone who's spiritually dead cannot enlist in a spiritual army. He must first receive new life.

Notice the object of faith we're emphasizing when we tell others they must give their lives to Christ in order to be saved. Their faith is being directed toward *what I must do for Christ* rather than what Christ has done for me.

Over the years I've talked to several people who "gave their lives to Christ" but never became Christians. How is that possible? In each case their faith was resting on what they had done for God (self-surrender), not on what He had done for them in giving His Son.

We haven't given people the true gospel until we point out a Person to receive and fully trust, rather than a lifestyle to follow. Once they receive that Person, He immediately infuses them with the desire and power for the new lifestyle He requires.

HOW WE VIEW OTHERS

This new purity has momentous impact on how I view others. It tells me, for example, that there are no insignificant believers. Each one's worth is forever secured by the blood of Christ shed for them.

Once Paul was captured by Christ, he forever saw believers in light of their divine purity, not their sinful flesh. Acknowledging that some of the Corinthian believers had been "fornicators," "idolaters," "adulterers," "homosexuals," "thieves," "covetous," "drunkards," "revilers," and "extortioners," he immediately affirms, "But *you were washed,* but *you were sanctified,* but *you were justified* in the name of the Lord Jesus and by the Spirit of our God" (1 Corinthians 6:9-11). Our new

---

FAITH'S FOUNDATION STONE

"The bedrock of our Christian faith is the unmerited, fathomless marvel of the love of God exhibited on the cross of Calvary, a love we never can and never will merit."

—Oswald Chambers

---

purity enables me to view myself and all other believers through the new lenses of imputed righteousness.

It also reminds me that no unbeliever should be dismissed as worthless. "God has shown me," Peter said, "that I should not call any man common or unclean" (Acts 10:28). The most obnoxious, hateful, irritating heathen is still someone Christ came to die for. God calls me to pray for them, serve them, and strive for their acceptance of Christ's death.

11. What can make it difficult to view others in this appropriate way? And how do you think such difficulties could be overcome?

SECURE ENOUGH TO LOVE

We begin taking the risks that genuine love requires—and launching out into the joyous adventure of such love—only when our own hearts are resting securely in a surplus of love that can never be removed. Our God-bestowed security is the foundation for loving others well.

Only secure people can love well. Only through the God-bestowed security of our new purity can our souls be freed from enslavement to others' acceptance and approval.

It's only natural that I *desire* your acceptance; there's nothing wrong or sinful in that. But when I cease deriving my full acceptance from Christ, I'll begin to *require* and *strive* for your acceptance. To the degree I do that, I'm incapacitated from loving you well.

This insecurity may exhibit itself in a pushy, grasping style of relating that openly criticizes your not being more caring toward me. Or it may come through in a quiet fear, refusing to ruffle feathers lest your acceptance of me be jeopardized. In either case, my ability to love you fully is sabotaged.

All this is why it's so important to feast constantly on God's love as seen at the cross. As we profoundly sense our own forgiveness and acceptance, we'll be released to freely extend the same toward others.

12. Take a moment to prayerfully evaluate your own experience of resting securely in God's love, forgiveness, and acceptance. Can you recognize any blocks to that experience at this time in your life? How would you express what these might be?

Before we move on to the second great provision of the New Covenant, I encourage you to evaluate how God's gift of your new purity is affecting your life, especially your view toward others and your relationships with them. Are you living enough in the rich and grateful experience of God's grace to impart this same grace to others? *Only grace-soaked saints can become grace-dispensing servants.*

13. To what degree do you think you can describe yourself already as a "grace-soaked saint"? What, if anything, seems to keep you from more fully experiencing this grace?

OPTIONAL FURTHER STUDY (FOR GOING IN-DEPTH)— GRACE AND FAITH

1. *Study closely any of the following passages to help you answer this question as best you can: What are the most important and foundational things that God wants us to understand about His grace? Be especially open to getting a wider perspective on this than you've had in the past.*

    Matthew 11:28-30; 20:1-16; Romans 3:21-24; 5:12-21; 2 Corinthians 8:9; Ephesians 2:1-10

2. *Study closely any of the following passages to help you answer this question as best you can: What are the most important and foundational things God wants us to understand about faith?*

    Genesis 15:1-6; John 11:11-44; 14:5-14; 20:24-31; Romans 4:1-25; Hebrews 11:1-40; James 2:14-26

Releasing Your New Identity

The moment I consider Christ and myself as two, I am gone.

MARTIN LUTHER

(As you begin, remember again to ask for the Holy Spirit's help in hearing and welcoming and obeying His words for you at this time.)

There's a Native American fable about a young brave who happened upon a nest of golden eagle eggs. Deciding to have some fun, he took one of the eggs and placed it in the nest of some prairie chickens.

The egg hatched, and the changeling eagle grew up with the brood of prairie chickens. Believing himself to be like everyone else around him, he behaved accordingly. He clucked and cackled and scratched in the dirt for seeds and insects to live on. He never flew more than a few feet off the ground, since prairie chickens are incapable of rising any higher.

Years passed. One day the young eagle was scratching along with one of his older prairie chicken brothers when a fleeting shadow passed over them. They looked up and saw, high in the sky, the soaring form of something gliding on the currents of the wind.

"What a beautiful bird!" the young eagle exclaimed.

"That's an eagle," the older brother informed him, staring upward. "A golden eagle. He's the king of the air. No bird can compare with him." Then he lowered his gaze and added, "But don't give it a second thought; you could never be like him."

And back to scratching they went. Indeed, the changeling eagle never gave another thought to that soaring sight. According to the fable, he died as he had lived, never rising any higher than a prairie chicken's existence.

Tragically, this same story is repeated in the lives of far too many believers. Like eagles, we were created and redeemed to mount up on God-given wings. Our privileged calling is to breathe deeply the crisp and rarified air of knowing our God more and more intimately…to know the keen thrill of unrestrained, exuberant worship…and to abandon ourselves to the high adventure of warring on behalf of God's kingdom in this dark world.

This is our God-given design—and that's why we cannot truly be satisfied with anything less. We can never find the intense fulfillment our souls yearn for while scratching around in carnal living or mediocre spirituality. We were made—*and fully equipped at the time of our conversion*—to soar.

What we'll explore in this lesson is simply the abiding joy of falling in line with our true design. We'll discover many surprising and life-changing realities…to the glory of God, whose lavish grace makes this kind of soaring truly attainable.

1. Think about your "true design" as you now understand it. How would you summarize what that design is?

Risky Business

In the last lesson we saw that grace is risky business. It's also the most soul-intoxicating, life-transforming commodity in the universe. Nothing rivals its ability to turn sinners into saints. Unfortunately, it can also be abused by saints who continue trafficking in sin. Surely God has erected some safeguards or barriers to keep us from taking advantage of His good nature.

But we saw that when Paul addressed this thorny issue of why we should not "continue in sin that grace may abound" (Romans 6:1), he did not erect a safeguard. Instead he laid a foundation to launch us into holiness. That foundation is the radical, actual new personhood gifted us at our conversion. It's time to explore in depth that new personhood.

First we'll discover that *we're no longer who we used to be.* Equally we'll find that *we're now what we never were.* Grace has permanently changed not only our eternal destiny but also our present identity.

Three Fundamental Changes

Let's quickly get the big picture here. At conversion three things were radically altered simultaneously.

2. What happened to us *legally,* according to Colossians 2:13-14?

3. What happened to us *relationally,* according to Romans 8:15-16?

4. What happened to us *inherently*—that is, in our deepest internal nature—according to 2 Corinthians 5:17?

What happened to us at our conversion? Legally, we went from being guilty before an infinitely holy God to being fully forgiven and acquitted of all crimes. Relationally, we went from being condemned slaves to adopted children. And there was a radical change as well in our deepest internal nature. We went from being "by *nature* children of wrath" (Ephesians 2:3) to being "partakers of the *divine nature*" (2 Peter 1:4).

The intrinsically wicked part of us is now offset (not removed) by an intrinsically perfect nature belonging to God Himself. Our *condition* has changed as well as our *position*. We're now thoroughly renovated saints.

WHAT NO PILL CAN DO

Imagine a courtroom where a newly convicted criminal is standing, about to be sentenced for his crimes. Suddenly the judge looks away from the criminal and calls his own son to the bench. The gavel comes crashing down, and the judge pronounces the criminal "not guilty" because his son has agreed to serve the sentence in full. This represents, of course, the first aspect of our conversion: justification. Our legal debt before God has been paid in full.

Then the judge steps down from the bench, puts His arm around the criminal, and tells him he wants to adopt him into his family. "You're coming home with us," the judge says warmly. This is the next aspect of our conversion: our adoption.

But the third aspect of our conversion—our inner renovation—is something no human judge could ever possibly do. The criminal may walk out of that courtroom forgiven and adopted, but he's still fundamentally the same person as before.

There's no pill the judge can give him to cause the criminal to actually *want* to do right from now on, something to offset the man's criminal inclinations.

Yet this is exactly what God has done in our rebirth. We're changed *inherently* as well as legally and relationally. "Christ is made unto us inherent as well as imputed righteousness," wrote Jonathan Edwards.

5. What brought about this inherent change, according to Paul's words in Titus 3:5?

COSTUME JEWELRY OR TARNISHED SILVER?

Costume jewelry is essentially worthless metal covered with an attractive coating. So many believers see themselves in that way—sinners through and through, yet covered by the blood of Christ.

Tarnished silver is a much truer image of who we are after conversion. While we're covered by the infinite righteousness of Christ, we're also new creations in Christ (silver) clothed in an earth suit that is sin-saturated (tarnished). The new you isn't a sinner but rather a saint who struggles with the tarnish of sin. We're golden eagles with prairie-chicken tendencies still hanging on.

6. (a) How do you respond to the major observations and conclusions mentioned so far in the text of this lesson? Do you find yourself disagreeing with them in any way? If so, how would you explain these points of disagreement?

(b) How does 1 Corinthians 6:9-11 relate to or illustrate these points?

(c) As God's people, our active and actual sharing in His righteousness (and the peace that accompanies it) is an engaging theme in many prophetic passages that point to the New Covenant. Explore some of the following passages to see how this is expressed, and record your findings.

Isaiah 1:26; 26:1-3; 54:13-14,17; 60:21; 61:3,10; 61:11; 62:1-3; Jeremiah 23:5-6; 33:15-16; Hosea 2:19-20; Malachi 3:3

One night my wife and I were having a fairly heated discussion over a particular habit of mine that annoyed her. As the discussion continued, I became angrier and more defensive, a reaction Sandy didn't understand.

Finally I realized I was attaching her criticisms to my essential identity, which was causing me to feel threatened. However, it wasn't *me* she was finding fault with, but only a particular behavior of mine.

God brought a picture to my mind. "So," I told Sandy, "it's not like you're saying I'm ugly, but just pointing out that my hair's out of place."

"That's *exactly* what I'm saying," she responded. She went on to again affirm my true identity (something she's so good at), which made it much easier for me to hear her comments about my annoying habit.

This picture has helped me many times since then. As Christians we all have our hair out of place in different ways, but *no believer is fundamentally ugly.* That's true because, at our conversion, we received far more than forgiveness and a new eternal destiny; we also received an internal, unalterable *transformation.* A supernatural revolution within has occurred. You're not merely a forgiven sinner; you're a "new creation" (2 Corinthians 5:17)—though certainly there's plenty of room for growth as new creations.

Remember the golden eagle? As long we view ourselves fundamentally as sinners (though forgiven), then soaring, saintly living will appear over our heads and out of reach; we'll stay trapped in prairie-chicken living.

7. (a) How have you primarily viewed yourself? As a forgiven sinner but still a sinner through and through? Or as a renovated saint? What has caused you to view yourself the way you have?

(b) How did Paul primarily view himself? Look at Romans 7:17-22 to form your answer. What was primary in Paul's new identity—sin or righteousness?

What's truly *primary* to us as believers is our divinely implanted righteousness; sin is now only secondary. "Saintness" is not only your position (through justification and adoption), it's also your condition. "Saintness" is your state as well as your status. Sin is still resident in our overall condition, but it's no longer the primary homeowner.

Therefore, "The Christian life is simply the process of becoming who we are," as someone ably expressed it. We don't change our living in order to become godly; we change our living because we've already been made godly. We stop scratching around like prairie chickens, not in order to *become* golden eagles, but because we really *are* golden eagles. In Christ we're *complete* (Colossians 2:10), though not yet *completed.*

SWALLOWED UP

This new identity is entirely ours because of our union with Christ.

8. After Paul declared (in 1 Corinthians 1:30), "You are *in* Christ Jesus," he immediately summarized what Christ Himself "became for us." Look up this passage.

(a) What has Jesus Himself specifically become for us?

(b) How could a deep understanding of this passage help us when we feel incompetent in grasping biblical truth?

(c) How could it help when we primarily view ourselves as unworthy and sinful?

(d) How could it help when we're sensing that the Christian life requires too much of us?

(e) How could it help when we feel trapped in difficult circumstances?

This is a passage to feast on. Hear the opening words again: *You are in Christ Jesus.* Our new identity is *a Christ-saturated identity.* As believers we no longer have the option of thinking of ourselves as separate from Him. We're wholly swallowed up in Him.

"Your life," Paul says, "is hidden with Christ in God," and Jesus Christ "*is* our life," he adds (Colossians 3:3-4). Our assimilation is so radical that it's virtually impossible to tell where we begin or He ends. He *is* our life and therefore the strength of our identity, its center and circumference.

JESUS OUR WISDOM

Our new identity is also *a Christ-sufficient identity.* All we'll ever need to live life as God designed it—*everything* for time and eternity—is supplied through our unbreakable union with Christ.

Do you see yourself as unskilled and unproductive in grasping the things of

God? Then remember Paul's words that Jesus Himself has become *your* "wisdom from God."

I first started truly walking with the Lord in my early twenties (tennis had been my whole life up to that point). As I began spending time with other committed believers, I easily became intimidated by the amount of Bible knowledge and spiritual wisdom they evidenced. They knew all kinds of passages by heart; about the only thing I knew was that Jesus loved me. Their Bibles were falling apart from use, and some had even had their Bibles rebound, which to me was almost unbelievable. I wrestled with deep feelings of spiritual inferiority as I compared myself to them.

One night during that time I was trying to study my Bible but feeling little sense of progress. I lowered my forehead to my desk and prayed something to the effect, "Lord, you know I'm nothing but a dumb jock. I just can't get what everyone else seems to get. If I'm going to know You or gain any wisdom, You're going to have to *give* it to me, because I clearly can't get it on my own."

Only years later did I discover that understanding the Scriptures spiritually, not just academically, is impossible apart from Christ's presence and the ministry of His Spirit. But from that night on, any spiritual wisdom I've gleaned over the years from Scripture has always felt far more like a gift than an acquisition. Certainly I've tried to study diligently and utilize the original languages. But every significant discovery has come chiefly through desperate reliance on Christ to open my mind and heart.

I no longer see myself as dumb. I don't really think of myself as smart, either. I

> "You are so entirely joined unto Christ, that He and you are made as it were one person; so that you may boldly say, 'I am now one with Christ,' that is to say, Christ's righteousness, victory, and life are mine."
>
> —Martin Luther

see myself simply as someone merged with the wisdom of Christ, enjoying what God has given me while recognizing that an endless ocean of His wisdom still lies before me.

GETTING USED TO JUSTIFICATION

Do you see yourself as unworthy and sinful? Then remember Paul's declaration that Jesus Himself has become *your righteousness.* In God's eyes you're whiter than the freshly fallen snow and purer than the clearest stream.

The righteousness of God not only covers you but also indwells you. Paul describes this as "being *filled* with the fruits of righteousness which are by Jesus Christ, to the glory and praise of God" (Philippians 1:11), and he states that our present experience of the kingdom of God means "righteousness and peace and joy in the Holy Spirit" (Romans 14:17). Does the Christian life seem to require too much of you? Do His commands seem utterly overwhelming? Then remember God's affirmation that Jesus Himself has become *your sanctification.*

This sanctification is a gift as well as a process. When we're born again, we receive a new nature that's already sanctified; the *process* of sanctification is merely the ongoing unveiling of this gifted sanctification. Someone put it like this: "Sanctification is simply the art of getting used to justification."

Do you see yourself as being in such difficult circumstances that you have no hope of being delivered? Then remember God's truth that Jesus Himself has become *your redemption.* He provides, as Edwards said, "actual deliverance from all misery, and the bestowment of all happiness and glory."

A RELAXED SELF-IMAGE

This inexhaustible sufficiency of Christ is what allows us to have a joyful and relaxed self-image, one that isn't grasping for proof of personal adequacy. Our sense of self is now God-derived, God-sustained, God-absorbed, God-glorifying. What frees us from the paralyzing grip of inferiority and inadequacy is not the power of positive thinking but the wonder of united identity with Christ.

What we experience is not better *self-esteem* but genuine *Christ-esteem.* We humbly enjoy our new identity and thank God for it. Yet we glory not in *it,* but in *the Lord* who gave it. After Paul tells us that Christ Himself has become our wisdom and righteousness and sanctification and redemption, he draws our attention to the higher purpose—"that, as it is written, 'He who glories, let him glory in the LORD'" (1 Corinthians 1:31). All the recognition for our new identity must go to Christ.

UNITED WITH CHRIST

9. In Romans 6:4-11, Paul identified different aspects of Christ that we become "united" with at our conversion. List these, and describe your best understanding of the significance of each.

FORGET IMPROVING YOUR SELF-IMAGE?

Why should we not be preoccupied with developing a good self-image?

Because we already have the best one available!

"God has given us something far more fascinating to think about than ourselves," as Oswald Chambers once put it. We're to be preoccupied with the beauty and "spectacularness" of Christ and how we can best display it in everyday living.

With Him in Death

When we trust Christ for salvation, we become indissolubly united with Christ in four dimensions of His existence.

First, we become united with Him *in His death* on the cross two thousand years ago. This is what Paul meant in saying, "I have been crucified with Christ" (Galatians 2:20). *You* also died on that cross at Calvary; we're "born crucified" (in L. E. Maxwell's words) when we become Christians.

Do you find this difficult to comprehend? It's not difficult; it's *impossible*. But we don't have to wholly understand it to experience it, just as I drive my car each day without fully understanding most of what makes it work. We simply need to trust that we've shared in Christ's death, because God says so.

Our death on the cross with Christ is what sets *us* free from sin's power and dominion over us. "Our old man was crucified with Him," Paul says, "that the body of sin might be done away with, that we should no longer be slaves of sin" (Romans 6:6). The Greek word translated here as "done away with" could be better expressed as "rendered inoperative" or "put out of business." The point is not that sin is *eradicated* but *incapacitated*.

It's not that sin has ceased to be real and very present, but it has ceased to be the inevitable master. Sin's power over us was "put out of business" when we died with Christ on His cross. Temptations are no problem for dead people.

But while we've died to sin, *nowhere does the Scripture say that sin has died to us.* The fundamental meaning of death is "separation." Because of our death with Christ we've become separated from sin's power, although that power is in no way extinguished. We can still choose to reconnect ourselves to sin's dominion, but the cross has given us the freedom to choose otherwise. This is why Scripture commands, "Reckon yourselves to be dead indeed to sin" (Romans 6:11). Our responsibility is not so much to mortify the flesh as to remember our death and act upon it. Ruth Paxson put it well: "Sin need have no more power over the believer than he grants it through unbelief. If he is alive unto sin it will be due largely to the fact that he has failed to reckon himself dead unto sin."

10. How would you explain or restate the truth that we're one with Christ "in the likeness of His death" (Romans 6:5) in a way that has the most personal application to you at this time?

BURIED WITH HIM

We're also united with Christ in His burial—"Therefore we were buried with Him through baptism into death" (Romans 6:4), as Paul expressed it. We're merged into Christ's experience in the tomb. God has buried the old us with His Son. This, too, is why we aren't the same people coming out of conversion that we were going in. The people we were before are left inside the tomb with the graveclothes. "Old things have passed away," Paul said; "behold, all things have become new" (2 Corinthians 5:17).

We're no longer who we used to be. Let those words sink deeply into your soul. God's way of dealing with our past is not recovery, but *burial.* This is why the "fix what is wrong" model is inherently flawed. God has no intention of fixing what He has buried.

If you were an alcoholic going into conversion, you weren't one when you came out. You may still struggle with alcohol, even intensely, but in your essential personhood you are *not* an alcoholic. You're a new creation in Christ whose flesh is especially tempted by drink, but the real you is "created according to God, in true righteousness and holiness" (Ephesians 4:24).

If you were the victim of a dysfunctional home (who isn't, to one degree or another?), your victim-identity did not remain intact after regeneration. It was shredded at the cross. You may still struggle in your flesh with the effects of your

---

OLD THINGS, NEW THINGS

What are some of the "old things" that have "passed away" for us (as 2 Corinthians 5:17 expresses it) simply as a result of our becoming Christians? Here are just a few:

- Our old identity as a sinner
- Sin's control over us
- Our guilt over past sins

And what are some of the "new things" that now are ours? Again, here are just a few:

- We're new creations.
- We're partakers (partners) in God's nature.
- We're blessed with every spiritual blessing in heaven.
- We're complete in Christ.
- We're the fragrance of Christ.
- We're Christ's workmanship.
- We're heirs of God.
- We're children of God.
- We're indwelt by Christ.
- We're more than conquerors.

(See 2 Corinthians 2:15; 5:17; Romans 6:1-14; 8:16-17,37; Galatians 2:20; Ephesians 1:3; 2:10; Colossians 1:27; 2:10-14; 3:3; 2 Peter 1:4.)

---

home life. But your true identity has nothing to do with past dysfunction and everything to do with present Christ-oneness. In Christ you actually have *a new past, a new family* (the body of Christ), and *a new Father.*

Whatever the reality of your own past, it's no longer the deepest reality of your present. Your background is buried with Christ.

11. How would you explain or restate the truth that we're "buried with Christ" in a way that has the most personal application to you at this time?

RESURRECTED WITH HIM

The third dimension is our union with Christ's resurrection—"united together...in the likeness of His resurrection" (Romans 6:5). "You were raised with Christ," Paul stated (Colossians 3:1). We're inseparably united to the same power that raised Christ from the dead.

Through our crucifixion and burial with Christ, we're no longer who we used to be; through union with His resurrection *we now are who we never were.* Every believer is a walking miracle, the scene of resurrection power. This is why Paul said, "Just as Christ was raised from the dead by the glory of the Father, even so we also should walk in newness of life" (Romans 6:4).

Whatever God calls us to in this life is to be carried out in reliance upon the Lord's grave-busting power, a power that's always present.

12. How would you explain or restate the truth that we're "resurrected with Christ" in a way that has the most personal application to you at this time?

STILL ALIVE, STILL AT WORK

The fourth dimension is our union with Christ's present life. "It is no longer I who live," Paul wrote, "but *Christ lives* in me" (Galatians 2:20).

We're united with One who not only has a perfectly stellar past but also a perfectly stellar present. Christ didn't stop living for God after He was resurrected and ascended; He's at work on earth (through His Spirit and His people), and He's at work in heaven, where "He always lives to make intercession for them" (Hebrews 7:25). Christ right now is living as fully and working as passionately for His Father's glory as ever. This fully engaged Christ now dwells within us, One with whom we're supernaturally incorporated. We live unto God because we're one with Him who never stops living for His Father. We've simply come along for the ride, so to speak.

Our life is not trying to "live for" Christ; our life *is* Christ Himself. This is why

> *I need not journey far, this distant Friend to see;*
>
> *Companionship is always mine; He makes His home with me.*
>
> *I envy not the twelve; closer to me is He;*
>
> *The life that once He lived on earth, He lives again in me.*
>
> —Anonymous

the New Covenant was given: Christ for our past, Christ for our present, Christ for our future.

In Christ's death and burial we find God's provision for our *past* identity; in Christ's resurrection and life we find His provision for our *present* identity.

13. How would you explain or restate the truth that we're "united with Christ's present life" in a way that has the most personal application to you at this time?

THE RIGHT PATH

This radical, actual new personhood given to us at conversion is our true foundation for godly living. Paul's essential message in Romans 6 is this: We ought no longer live the way we used to live *because we are no longer who we used to be.* After Paul explained our justification (in Romans 5), he took pains (in chapters 6 and 7) to show us what it means specifically to be a new creation in Christ *before* moving on to talk about the Holy Spirit's role in our sanctified living (chapter 8).

So often in the church today we try to rush people immediately from Romans 5 to Romans 8 and bypass the message of Romans 6 and 7. But after recognizing our new purity (justification), God wants us to focus next on our new identity. Then we'll see all of life in a new light. We won't view God's commands merely as a list of "should's" but as trails leading to a soul satisfaction and personal significance found nowhere else on earth.

14. As you give attention to all that's true about your new identity, take a moment to fully express this in praise and worship to Jesus, your Lord and Savior—who *is* your life (Colossians 3:4). Record your worship prayer here:

OPTIONAL FURTHER STUDY (FOR GOING IN-DEPTH)—OUR UNITY WITH CHRIST

1. *What further aspects of our union or identity with Christ are presented in the following passages? Explore each one and record your findings.*
   1 Corinthians 2:16; Ephesians 5:23-24; Philippians 4:7; 1 Peter 2:4-5; 1 John 3:2-3

2. As God's people, the church is sometimes spoken of as the "bride" of Christ. Explore how this image is touched on by God's Word in the following passages. How does this image relate to your own union and identity with Christ? Record your insights below.

Isaiah 54:5-8; Hosea 2:19-23; Ephesians 5:29-32; Revelation 19:7-8; 21:9

Your Newness Goes Public

God became man to turn creatures into sons; not simply to produce
better men of the old kind but to produce a new kind of man.

C. S. LEWIS

Fall in New England—there's nowhere I'd rather be to see the leaves changing colors. As someone who grew up among the more subdued hues of West Texas, I find few things on earth more stunningly beautiful than the brilliant red, orange, and yellow of the northeastern autumn landscape.

A few years ago I discovered something interesting about how those leaves change color. In essence, they don't. All spring and summer each leaf's true color is masked over by green chlorophyll cells. When fall comes and the chlorophyll departs, the true color is no longer obscured. The "change" is really just an unveiling. The leaf doesn't become more colorful; it shows the world what it has been all along.

That, my friend, is the essence of true spirituality. Christian growth—our sanctification—is the continued unveiling of the full array of our true colors, colors that were divinely and unalterably given us the instant we trusted Christ. These colors are nothing less than those of God Himself.

That's why our further maturing in Christ—our sanctification—is simply *becoming who we are,* as we said in the last lesson. Our life's story becomes the continuing saga of our new creation state going public. Let's now explore more deeply the practical ramifications of that unveiling.

Your Scar

A scientific researcher once got ten volunteers to participate in an experiment to study how people respond to a stranger with a physical deformity—in particular, an unsightly facial scar.

The experiment proceeded separately for each volunteer. A makeup artist applied the ugly "scar," then the person was shown his or her image in a hand-held mirror before being sent to a medical office waiting room to sit and observe people's reactions.

However, just before each person was sent out, the makeup artist deftly erased the scar altogether under the guise of applying a finishing touch of powder to keep the scar from smearing. None of the volunteers realized this last-second change. And all ten later reported the same kind of reactions in the waiting room: People were rude, shunned them, and kept staring at their scars!

More than we're aware, we view others and their responses to us through how we see ourselves. For believers, that picture is often quite inaccurate in light of God's truth.

Is God Telling the Truth About You?

The key issue for every believer is not whether our sense of identity is good or poor, but whether it's accurate. *What keeps us from fully believing that God is telling the truth when He describes the revolution within us at our conversion?*

1. Respond to that last question here, as fully as you can:

"You are *complete* in Him," Paul said in Colossians 2:10 about the practical result of our oneness in Christ. The Greek word here most literally means "having been made *full*." You've been literally filled with every resource for walking the path of discipleship.

2. Look up Colossians 2:9-10 as well as some of the following passages to meditate further on our completeness in Christ, and record your thoughts.
John 1:16-17; 1 Corinthians 3:21-23; Galatians 3:26-29; Colossians 3:9-11

GOD'S VERY NATURE WITHIN

This is why a good self-image is not *developed* but rather *received*. We aren't called to figure out new ways to think positively about ourselves, but to humbly and gratefully trust what God says about who we are in Christ. Our true identity is as much a gift from God as getting into heaven—and just as real. And it's ready *now* to be applied.

I just finished making a difficult phone call. It concerned a fairly messy and complicated situation with the potential of becoming ugly, and I felt wholly inadequate to handle it. I dreaded the call and kept putting it off all day.

What helped me most to finally dial the number was reminding myself of what God has placed within me. My inadequacies aren't all there is to me; within me there resides *God's very nature* of love, compassion, boldness, and wisdom, and this is actually more central to who I am than any of my shortcomings.

This was my sole hope for handling the call in a God-honoring fashion. I trusted God to provide what I needed to glorify Him and to love the person I would be talking with. With genuine reliance on Him, I made the call, although still a bit reluctantly.

How did it go? Okay. Not great. Not terrible. On the whole I felt I was simply releasing what God had put within me. There were times I felt my flesh coming into play and I became tentative, but overall my spoken words and tone seemed like God's doing. I don't know what the results of the call will be, but that's not the issue. I sensed God's flowing, and in that I rest gratefully.

TESTING YOUR SELF-IDENTITY

What keeps us from deeply tapping into our new identity?

One of our biggest hindrances is *labeling*. If I say to myself, "You're just a

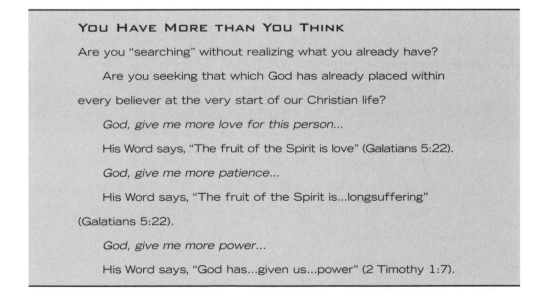

YOU HAVE MORE THAN YOU THINK

Are you "searching" without realizing what you already have?

Are you seeking that which God has already placed within every believer at the very start of our Christian life?

God, give me more love for this person...

His Word says, "The fruit of the Spirit is love" (Galatians 5:22).

God, give me more patience...

His Word says, "The fruit of the Spirit is...longsuffering" (Galatians 5:22).

God, give me more power...

His Word says, "God has...given us...power" (2 Timothy 1:7).

procrastinator," I'm labeling my fundamental identity. This is very different from saying, "You're procrastinating," which is honestly pointing out behavior without attacking identity.

Our only accurate labels are those we find in the Scriptures that portray our new identity—we're "in Christ," "a new creation," "partakers of the divine nature," "complete" in Christ, "the fragrance of Christ," Christ's "workmanship," "heirs of God," "children of God," "more than conquerors," and so on (1 Corinthians 1:30; 2 Corinthians 5:17; 2 Peter 1:4; Colossians 2:10; 2 Corinthians 2:15; Ephesians 2:10; Romans 8:17,16,37).

Is that how you most frequently see yourself? Or are you guilty of sticking on wrong labels?

3. Here's a test. Ask yourself this question: What role, responsibility, or aspect of my life has the potential to trigger in me the deepest disappointment as well as the highest happiness?

If you're a parent, your answer to the above question might be your children's behavior more than anything else that can cause you either to soar with pride or die of embarrassment. If so, your primary identity label is probably that of a mother or father. Your children's conduct then becomes the real barometer of your personal worth and significance, and you may find yourself trying to control your children rather than releasing them in God's direction.

Here's another way to help pinpoint your primary sense of identity:

4. (a) Write your first and last names below, leaving plenty of space to the right after your last name.

(b) Now go back and fill in the blank space after your name with the word or phrase that comes first to mind after saying your name. Be brutally honest.

As you completed the last part of the above question, there's a good chance that whatever thought came first represents the self-identity you hold most deeply.

More Wrong Labels

What are the inadequate labels we most often put in that blank?

One of the most common (especially for men) is our occupation—mechanic, accountant, teacher, programmer. But God never intended our occupation to become our primary source of identity. If we do, we let occupation override *vocation*—our calling to glorify God as comprehensively as possible. If my own primary identity is that of "pastor," I'll be more concerned about the appearance and size of "my" church than about advancing God's kingdom. When someone leaves the church, my sense of personal worth will be at stake.

Asked what she did for a living, a woman answered, "I'm a disciple of Jesus Christ disguised as a secretary." She was finding her identity in the right place.

We can also gravitate to a host of other self-labels. For some, it's a personality type or temperament ("Type A," "high I," "melancholic"). For others, it's a psychological condition, an addiction, a disability, or a past hurt: "manic-depressive," "schizophrenic," "alcoholic," "codependent," "ADHD," "dyslexic," "incest victim," "broken-home victim"—the list is practically endless.

Such conditions and situations can be only too real, their pain only too piercing. There's adversity and tragedy in the backgrounds and present circumstances of countless Christians, and these deeply affect them. But the issue is this: Where has it affected them?

No Christian has a damaged soul. What we all have is wrinkled flesh—flesh in the sense of our fallen, sinful nature. Pain in our past leaves *no imprints whatsoever* on our new creation state, but it can cause our flesh to react in self-protective or self-gratifying ways.

This doesn't mean there's no place for looking at our past, but our purpose should be to find whatever hinders us from more fully appropriating our supernatural present. (We often need assistance in seeing the lies that block the way; a godly counselor or shepherd can be immeasurably helpful here.)

No Christian need ever stand up in an Alcoholics Anonymous meeting and declare, "I am an alcoholic." It simply isn't true. He may be struggling with alcohol addiction, but he himself is not an alcoholic. The real him is a new creation garbed in alcohol-craving flesh. The starting point for real victory is recognizing that his real identity thirsts for righteousness much more than for alcohol.

The same is true for all other addictions, as well as any mental or physical disabilities. No such limitation is a Christian's true identity. My son, who has cerebral palsy, is not a cerebral palsic (if there is such a word). He's a disciple of Jesus whose

---

WHO'S THERE?

Your bad habits, your personality profile, your "problems," your "tendencies"—these things are never your core identity. God has seen to it that something far better is at the center of your personhood.

"Should anyone knock at my heart," wrote Martin Luther, "and say, 'Who lives here?' I should reply, 'Not Martin Luther, but the Lord Jesus Christ.'"

There's no pride whatsoever in seeing yourself this way, for your new identity in Christ is wholly the work of God. And now God calls you to humbly and joyously embrace it.

---

temporary physical body doesn't move as well as most other people's bodies. His true identity isn't affected one iota by the disability God has entrusted him with on this earth.

5. How do you respond to the major observations and conclusions made in the preceding paragraphs? How fully do you agree with them? In what ways do you disagree?

Sin Labels

One of the most common labels with which Christians wrongly tag themselves is that of a sin—"adulterer," "drunkard," or whatever. As we genuinely take hold of who we are in Christ, we'll see our sin in a new light.

You'll recall my mention (at the beginning of this workbook) of Greg and his struggle with homosexuality. Greg told me that one day he was reading in 1 Corinthians 6—where Paul lists homosexuality and several other sins of the Corinthians. When his eyes fell on the words, "and such *were* some of you," a light went on in his heart. For the first time he realized that now he *is not* a homosexual but a new creation in Christ whose flesh happens to struggle with homosexuality. This realization, more than anything else, led to Greg's truly remarkable and supernatural turnaround.

6. Think clearly and objectively about where you've been finding your primary sense of identity. Have you been tagging your deepest self with inadequate labels that are merely human, rather than the spiritual labels God has provided through your new creation in Christ? Record your assessment here:

WEAPONS FOR THE WAR

The story is told of a man on a psychiatrist's couch who explained, "When I go grocery shopping and walk past the dog food section, I have this overwhelming urge to rip open an Alpo bag and start eating."

SOMEONE NEW AND DIFFERENT

Before Augustine of Hippo was converted to Christianity, he was very immoral sexually. The story is told that, not long after he'd become a believer, he was walking down a side street when a woman came up quietly behind him. "Augustine, it is I," she whispered; he recognized her as someone with whom he'd been sexually involved.

Augustine turned to her and replied, "Yes, but it is not I." He knew he was no longer the man he used to be.

So it is for every believer. When we don't recognize this truth, the results are tragic.

Here was something the doctor had never encountered. He asked when his patient first began noticing this urge.

"I'm not really sure," the man replied. "I think ever since I was a puppy."

I know it's a dumb joke, but it makes an important point. If you believe you're a dog, dog food will seem both reasonable and necessary. And if you believe you're still fundamentally a sinner, *sin will seem both reasonable and necessary.* When sin feels inevitable, it's almost always because we aren't in tune with our true identity.

7. (a) Think again about that last sentence. Would you say this is usually the case when you face strong temptation to sin?

(b) Reflect on Colossians 3:1-10. How does our true identity affect how we can deal with sin in our lives?

Our union with Christ provides freedom from sin's shackles. Sin has become genuinely unnecessary. It's now an option rather than a certainty. Sin is not lust encountered, but lust obeyed.

Sin is also utterly inappropriate to our new identity. Having been supernaturally renovated to "walk in newness of life" (Romans 6:4), we're now to display our new wardrobe of divine royalty. To continue living in sin would be like the queen of England going around in the tattered and dirty garb of a bag lady.

Furthermore, sin is wholly insane because of our new identity. Paul said of sin,

"The end of those things is death" (Romans 6:21). No matter what sin promises up front, it always brings a deadening to our lives—loss of joy, loss of peace, fear of being found out, and so on. I like John Piper's definition of sin as "the suicidal abandonment of joy." Until we understand that our sin is as *foolish* as it is *wrong*, we probably won't change.

8. How are you viewing sin? Are you continuing in any sins because you haven't seen them as truly unnecessary in your life, fully inappropriate, and entirely foolish? Record your honest assessment here:

BENEATH THE RABBIT

Every believer is a new creation, holy and righteous—what Charles Hodge defines as "my real and lasting self." Yet this real you, the new creation, is clothed in an earth-suit composed of sinful flesh.

C. S. Lewis pictured our old self, our earth-suit of flesh, as a rabbit:

"All the rabbit in us is to disappear—the worried, conscientious, ethical rabbit as well as the cowardly and sensual rabbit. We shall bleed and squeal as the handfuls of fur come out; and then, surprisingly, we shall find underneath it all a thing we have never yet imagined: a real Man...a son of God, strong, radiant, wise, beautiful, and drenched in joy."

9. What scriptures do you know that help you to understand the foolishness of sin? (A few suggestions: Proverbs 5:1-11; 20:17; Isaiah 55:2; Jeremiah 2:13.) And how have you seen the foolishness of sin in your own experience?

LIKE ANGELS INSIDE

Everything we've seen about labeling ourselves is just as true in how we view other believers.

This is especially so for our children who are saved. I was having a heated discussion one evening with one of my sons about why we needed a filtered Internet provider for our home computer. It makes Internet access extremely slow, but I explained the dangers (particularly the sexual ones) of not having a filter. With three teenage boys, the testosterone level at our house is off the chart anyway; no need to add fuel to the fire.

CHOCOLATE-COVERED ALPO

Sin for the believer is nothing better than chocolate-covered Alpo. It may bring momentary pleasure, but the aftertaste will kill you.

To go for Alpo when the choicest steak is available is foolish beyond words. Until we understand that sin is as foolish as it is wrong, we probably won't change.

Nothing helps us see that better than grabbing hold of who we really are now that Christ indwells us.

My son wasn't buying that. Frustrated with my reasoning, he finally said, "Dad, the problem is that you really don't trust me, do you?"

"Son," I answered, "I trust *you*. I really do. But I don't trust your hormones."

His demeanor changed immediately. The anger seemed to evaporate. He felt less threatened and could look at himself more objectively. We continued our conversation productively, admitting that neither of us can trust our own hormones.

One of the greatest gifts we can give other Christians, including our believing children, is to affirm their new identity continually and never confuse it with their flesh. Michelangelo once was asked where he got the inspiration for his famous sculpture of David. He spoke of a piece of marble that others had cast off and said, "I saw an angel trapped inside." This is how we're to see one another. We all have rough edges, but Christ dwells inside each of us, awaiting full release.

"We are not human beings having a spiritual experience," as someone has noted; "we're spiritual beings having a human experience."

OPTIONAL FURTHER STUDY (FOR GOING IN-DEPTH)—SIN AND RIGHTEOUSNESS

1. Study carefully Romans 6:15-23.

(a) According to this passage, what is your fundamental identity as a believer in Christ?

(b) How should you respond to that truth, according to this passage?

(c) What do you think this means in practical, everyday terms for you?

(d) What is the right way for you to view sin, according to this passage?

2. *How do the following passages help us gain a proper perspective regarding sin? What are the most important and fundamental views God wants us to have of sin?*

 Psalm 51:1-6; Matthew 15:10-20; John 8:21-34,44; Romans 2:12; 5:12-14; 7:7-25; 1 John 1:5-10; 2:1-2; 3:4-9

Releasing Your New Disposition

When the law is written in the heart…it means that the love of God's
law and of Himself has now become the moving power of our life.…
However cold or feeble we may feel, faith knows that the new heart is in
us, that the love of God's law is our very nature, that the teaching and
power of the Spirit are within us. Such faith knows it can obey.

ANDREW MURRAY

Liver is one of my least favorite foods. My problem is with the taste, or perhaps distaste is a better way to put it. I grew up dreading those nights Mom fixed liver for dinner, encouraging us with, "It's good for you." Those words meant nothing to me, and they certainly did nothing to make liver more palatable.

I've tried smothering it with ketchup or gulping it down with a bite of something else on my plate, but the liver flavor always seemed stronger than everything else. Nothing has ever come close to helping me like it.

I doubt that liver itself will ever be radically and substantively changed to taste like steak or hamburger. So for me to actually enjoy eating it, only one option seems to remain. I suppose it's conceivable that I could undergo a tongue transplant and be given the tongue of a liver-lover. My new set of taste buds could then rejoice in liver rather than merely endure it. Liver would no longer be an "ought to" but a "get to."

When you and I became believers, something similar happened to us. We were given a heart transplant that instilled a whole new set of God-given desires. God has seen to it that our new, regenerate hearts will incessantly and instinctively yearn for the best things in all the universe—Himself and His glory, His will and His words. This is every saint's innate longing, a hunger that goes unsatisfied at any other table but God's.

It's "a holy, heavenly disposition," as Jonathan Edwards termed it. Because of it, the will of God isn't just an "ought to" anymore, but also a "want to." Because of our revolution within, obeying Him has become not only our moral duty, but also our new heart's truest and deepest delight.

In this lesson we'll explore one of the most powerful yet overlooked *motivations*

OBEDIENCE FALSE AND TRUE

There are two kinds of obedience:

There's a kind of obedience that actually *quenches* the Spirit, and a kind of obedience that absolutely *requires* the Spirit (Galatians 3:3).

There's a kind of obedience that actually *distances* us from God, and a kind of obedience that *deepens* us with God (Galatians 4:9; 5:4).

There's a kind of obedience that *obscures* the beauty of Christ and a kind of obedience that *unveils* the beauty of Christ (Galatians 6:13-15).

"But now we have been delivered from the law, having died to what we were held by, so that we should serve in the newness of the Spirit and not in the oldness of the letter" (Romans 7:6).

for godly living, and one of the most liberating truths I've ever learned. It's the great reality that the desire to do the will of God is the gift of God.

1. In Philippians 2:12-13, look carefully at Paul's words to the believers at Philippi.

   (a) What is it that God Himself provides for us, according to this passage? Explain your understanding of this as fully as you can.

   (b) How does this provision from God relate to your own desire to obey and please Him? Is there ever a time when God gives us the power to do His will but not the desire?

   (c) Because of what God has provided, what are we to do, according to this passage? Explain this in your own words.

FOR OUR HEART OF STONE

We were born into the world with a disposition innately opposed to God. Spiritually, it's what Scripture describes as a "heart of stone" (Ezekiel 36:26)—cold, unyielding, lifeless. It's captivated by foolish thinking and controlled by wayward lusts, so that we're "alienated from the life of God" (Ephesians 4:18). Our thoughts, delights, and pursuits are out of alignment with His.

It's actually worse than simply being neutral toward God. "Enmity against God" (Romans 8:7), as Paul put it, is in fact the very heartbeat of our flesh. Our natural, inbred response toward God and His commands is distaste, anger, and undeniable rebellion. Jonathan Edwards described it as "an inbred distaste and disrelish of God's perfections."

2. Summarize the condition of our natural heart as it's described in Jeremiah 17:9 and Titus 3:3.

That's why God's New Covenant promise to His people through the prophet Ezekiel was this: "I will give you *a new heart*...a heart *of flesh*" (Ezekiel 36:26). To offset our natural heart of stone, this new heart is inclined and warm and responsive toward God and His righteousness—the kind of heart only God can give.

Earlier we faced the fact that God hasn't yet removed our old heart—our natural, sinful disposition. Even as we grow in Christ, that disposition can never be improved or reformed. There will never come a time when it loves, fears, or even tolerates God. At every turn our flesh despises Him, detests His rule, and yearns to do whatever He's forbidden. It obeys God only when it believes there will be greater personal benefit than if it disobeys. Till the day we die, it will be inclined toward levels of ungodliness that would cause us unspeakable shame if anyone knew what we were thinking.

The only remedy for our inbred hostility toward God is a supernatural invasion.

HEART ETCHING

These inclinations are within us because of God's New Covenant promise for His people: "I will put My law in their minds, and write it on their hearts" (Jeremiah 31:33).

NO LONGER SHOCKED

Even while preaching and performing weddings, I've had thoughts that shocked me with their hideous wickedness. I used to think a time would come when I'd be free from that; I'm now convinced it will never happen in this lifetime. I'm seldom surprised anymore at the degradation my flesh can stoop to and the thoughts it's capable of. But when this happens I try to remind myself of three things.

1. It isn't the real me producing such thoughts; it's my flesh. And for my flesh, such thoughts are merely par for the course.

2. The thought itself isn't sin, though my response to it can be. My responsibility is to not allow ungodly thoughts or temptation to find a welcome home within my soul.

3. There's something I desire far more at the core of my being than the sinful thought or the temptation at hand. Although it often doesn't feel this way at the moment, I always have a supernatural set of godly inclinations that *do* want to go God's direction. And so do you.

God hasn't altered His commands to fit our hearts; He has altered our hearts to fit His commands.

3. What it does it mean personally to you that God has written His law on your heart, as He promised in Jeremiah 31:33?

Describing this reality, Paul reminded the Corinthians that they were like an "epistle" or letter from Christ, in which the writing is "not on tablets of stone [as was true of the Old Covenant] but on tablets of flesh, that is, of *the heart*" (2 Corinthians 3:3). The Greek wording in this passage indicates a *permanent* etching within. And the place of that etching is our heart, the most central facet of our being. God went for the jugular, so to speak.

Paul also emphasized that this writing is supernatural—"not with ink but by the Spirit of the living God" (2 Corinthians 3:3). Our new disposition is never separate from the Holy Spirit. Were the Holy Spirit to leave us, our new disposition would vanish in the same instant. Thank God for His assurance that this will never happen!

Deeper than our sin, deeper than our pain, deeper than our fears is something clean, pure, and godly within us that ceaselessly yearns to know and reflect God. As Jonathan Edwards said, God's Spirit infuses within us "new, divine, and supernatural principles…vastly more noble and excellent than all that is in natural men."

> "The New Covenant is written on the fleshly tablets of the heart. Under its terms, the desire and ability to do God's will are incorporated into the believing man's inmost being. It becomes his second nature, the very spring of his choice and desires…. With his Master he is now able to say, 'I delight to do Thy will, O my God.'"
>
> —J. Oswald Sanders

The Lord, in effect, has made us liver lovers. We can do His will not only because it's good for us, but because it delights the taste buds of our new nature. The desire to do His will isn't something we have to work up but something to fall back on so that we say with the psalmist, "I delight to do Your will, O my God, and Your law is within my heart" (Psalm 40:8).

NEVER A BURDEN

These new inclinations for doing God's will were given to you *before* the light of Scripture ever brought any aspect of God's will to your attention. James calls it "the implanted word," which he tells us to "receive with meekness" (James 1:21). James is saying in essence, "Take hold of what you already have, that which is innate to your new nature." Ponder with your mind what God has already made your heart desire!

The birthright of every believer is an inner self that's supernaturally inscribed with the *whole* of Christ's teachings and commands—even to the extent that "we have the mind of Christ" (1 Corinthians 2:16), as Scripture says.

Every command we come across in the Bible is therefore a vigorous reminder to do what we already desire. The Scriptures simply clarify in our minds what we already want to do in our regenerate heart.

IT'S YOURS

"Grace not only saves the soul with an everlasting salvation, but it also imparts a nature which delights in everything that belongs to God, because it is divine.... Hence we do not put away evil from us in order to better our old nature, which is irremediable, nor yet to obtain the new nature, but because we have it. We have life, and in the power of that life, we put away evil."

—C. H. Mackintosh

What this means practically is that you'll never find a biblical command from God for which He hasn't already given you a desire to obey. Reading God's Word, we need never ask Him for the desire to do what we read; we thank Him for having already given us the desire, and we ask Him to help us appropriate it meaningfully.

4. Based on what you know of Scripture and of your own experience, how fully do you agree with the main point made in the preceding paragraph? Explain your response.

NO LONGER A BURDEN

Our new disposition to obey God must have been what the apostle John had in mind when he wrote in 1 John 5:3 that God's commands "are not burdensome." (Though I appreciate the honesty of Francis Schaeffer who said that for years he refused to preach on this passage because he had no idea what it meant! My guess is that many Christians, if they were honest, would say the same.)

Whatever John meant here, it applies to *all* of God's commands. He didn't say that "some" or even "most" of God's commandments "are not burdensome."

Love, for Example

As an example of one of these instinctive biblical commands, take the instruction to "love one another."

Paul told the Thessalonian believers, "Concerning brotherly love you have no need that I should write to you, for you yourselves are *taught by God* to love one another" (1 Thessalonians 4:9). Paul knew the Lord had already taken care of instructing them to love their fellow brethren. How did God do this? Not through external instruction, but through their internal desire.

I remember clearly experiencing this when I first became a believer. I was a high school senior at the time. Prior to my conversion I used to ridicule a group of "Jesus freak" students who held Bible studies on the steps of our high school at lunch. I joined my buddies in mocking them, saying, "Preach it, brother," and other things I now regret.

After I trusted Christ, the first time I passed by this group of Christian students, I sensed a fondness toward them that completely caught me off guard. It was as if I now was on their team, that we were somehow connected. Part of me (my flesh) couldn't believe this was happening; another part (my new disposition) couldn't deny the reality. Only years later did I realize from Scripture what had happened. Like the Thessalonians, I had been "taught by God" to love my fellow believers.

5. In your own experience, how have you seen that God has taught and inspired you to love other believers?

ANOTHER EXAMPLE: REMAINING SEXUALLY PURE

Another example of God's implanted Word is His command to remain sexually pure. Why should we obey this command? There are several good reasons, but one of the best, because of our new disposition, is something we often overlook. At the deepest level of our being, *we want to remain pure.* We want the joy of purity rather than the counterfeit pleasure of illicit sexuality.

6. In your own experience, how have you seen God teaching and inspiring you to desire the joy of purity?

The only way to overcome our lower passions is to glut our higher ones. Oswald Chambers reminds us, "Human nature, if it is healthy, demands excitement. And if it does not obtain its thrilling excitement in the right way, it will seek it in the wrong. God never made bloodless stoics; He makes passionate saints."

This is why it's important, when facing temptation, to ask ourselves not "What do I want?" but "What do I really want?" What do we as "passionate saints" desire at the deepest level of our being, not merely at the surface?

7. How would you fully answer that question at this very moment—What do I really want, at the deepest level of my being?

NO MORE HEART CHANGE NEEDED

I once received a brochure advertising a significant conference on ministry and leadership. As I opened it I noticed that one of the scheduled keynote speakers was a man I'd gone to seminary with and come to know fairly well.

I'd like to say my immediate response to seeing his name and picture was excitement for the opportunity God had given him. But that wasn't the case by a long shot. I found myself internally jealous that he, not I, had been asked to speak. Then I felt guilty, because he's a wonderful man of God who richly deserved to speak at the conference.

HERE'S YOUR STEAK

I spent so many years trying to muster up desire for what I knew God was requiring of me, or praying that God would change my heart. The good news, as we'll thoroughly investigate this week, is that *God has already changed* my heart, and yours as well.

For many years, as a pastor and teacher, I taught with the basic assumption that most of the people in front of me didn't really want to obey God's will. It was my job to try to coerce them into doing what they fundamentally didn't want to do. I call it now the "eat your vegetables" approach to ministry: You may not like what God commands, but go ahead and do it anyway because it's good for you.

Now I work from the basic assumption that, deep down, every true believer *does* want to do the will of God—though so many are unaware of this or are blocked in that realization. Now I try to minister from a "here's your steak" approach, helping others see all that they were created for and enticing the new appetite for righteousness that God placed in their souls at conversion.

As I began processing this before the Lord and confessing my sin, I asked Him to change my heart toward this brother and his ministry opportunity. Nothing seemed to happen. I began thinking of my past and present thought patterns and coping strategies that contributed to this sinful jealousy, but this only made my mood darker.

Then God gently reminded me there was something deeper in me than this jealousy. I began dwelling on the reality that God had written His law on my heart, that according to the New Covenant reality at the deepest core of my being, I *was* excited for this brother.

I began to sense faint stirrings of genuine gratitude for my brother's ministry. As I continued in this reflection, a clear joy for him continued to escalate in my heart. It was a joy I could take no credit for whatsoever; it was an implanted joy that God had deposited in my heart at conversion.

Instead of asking God to change my heart in that situation, what helped me most was fully remembering that God has *already* granted me a changed heart through His Spirit and that what I need most is to appropriate it.

8. To what extent can you see for yourself that what you need is not a change of heart, but simply to appropriate the change that has already happened? What questions, if any, does this point raise for you?

What Our New Heart Is Like

9. (a) What miracle has God done in our hearts, according to Romans 5:5?

(b) And what is the result of that miracle for us, according to 1 John 4:19?

(c) What do these truths mean practically for you?

The new heart God has given us is one that's warm toward Him, a heart inflamed with delight and affection for the One who so marvelously redeemed us, a heart that's soft and compliant toward commands.

It's a heart that loves God, just as He promised: "And the LORD your God will circumcise your heart…to love the LORD your God" (Deuteronomy 30:6). Love for God isn't something we're called to create, but to appropriate. Humbling as it may be to admit, none of us is born into this world with any genuine love toward God. Love for Him is the permanent, unshakable passion of the Holy Spirit within us. In other words, *we cannot love God unaided.*

10. Out of the new disposition that God has implanted in you, express here in a personal way your deepest love for Him.

Likewise, we cannot fear God unaided. Fearing Him is another gifted disposition granted to us at salvation. No one is born into the world with the ability to genuinely fear God. It must be given. Therefore God promised, "I will put My fear in their hearts so that they will not depart from Me" (Jeremiah 32:40). How hopeful this is for those of us who feel we don't honor and reverence the Lord as we should! We don't have to manufacture a proper fear for Him, but simply appropriate the indwelling, divinely placed fear already there. Certainly we're called to nourish and stimulate this fear, as well as our love for Him, but we're never adding to what's there, only bringing its fullness to the surface.

11. Out of the new disposition that God has implanted in you, express here in a personal way your deepest honor and reverence for Him.

Every aspect of our new disposition is something to be developed and nurtured, but it is and always will be the gift of God. We can never take credit for initiating any warmth toward God of any kind; it's provided through the Holy Spirit alone.

Even our heart to know God is a gift. "I will give them a heart to know Me," God promised in Jeremiah 24:7 as part of the New Covenant. These words from the book of Jeremiah have been of great spiritual help to me. When I feel dry and lifeless toward God, I remind myself of this reality. It isn't my responsibility to create a desire for knowing Him, but to fall back on the supernaturally implanted desire for knowing Him that was given me at conversion.

12. Again from the new disposition that God has implanted in you, express here in a personal way your deepest desire to know Him more fully.

IN DRY TIMES

During times of spiritual dryness, I ask God to point out what competing desires are keeping my deepest desire submerged. Almost always it has to do with idolatry in some form—ministry success, material security, approval of others, or something else.

As I confess these things and ask God to help me tap in to what He has placed within me, I normally sense the desire for knowing Him beginning to rise up.

OUR DESIRES AND OUR CONSCIENCE

How is this new disposition different from our conscience, the basic sense of right and wrong that all human beings have? After all, Paul affirms that even unbelievers have "the work of the law written in their hearts" (Romans 2:15).

But there's a distinction between "the *work* of the law" (or "the requirements of the law," as it's also translated) and the law itself. As Renald Showers explains in *The New Nature*, all unbelievers "have a moral consciousness, a sense of right and wrong, inherent within them," and this consciousness comes "as an inherent attribute of their total human nature."

But the New Covenant provides something totally different. When God actually writes His law in our hearts in the New Covenant sense, He makes His commands *instinctive* within us.

We see illustrations of a similar instinctiveness in nature. How do birds know exactly when and where to migrate for the winter? Do they take classes in southern migration? Obviously not. God has written His "migration law" on their hearts, so to speak. How did those same birds even learn to fly? It was because they followed a God-given instinct.

In the same way, righteousness, holiness, and love are the instinctive, innate desires of our new hearts, now that we're reborn. While many times these new inclinations don't feel real, that doesn't mean they aren't real. They're temporarily in hiding, lurking beneath the surface of competing inclinations that *seem* more alive at the time. The starting point for moving forward is to remember that our godless inclinations are only a part of the picture; the whole picture includes clean, pure, joyous inclinations toward the will of God.

These inclinations will never leave you or forsake you. At the deepest level of your being, *you always desire to do all the will of God.* There's never a time when you don't, never a situation where you don't. It certainly doesn't seem this way many times, but nonetheless it's true.

We must take it by faith. "The moment we believe God's promise and act upon it," J. Oswald Sanders writes, "We will find it true in experience."

13. As honestly as you can, express here your prayerful affirmation of faith that God has placed within you the permanent desire to do all His will.

STILL WONDERING?

You may still be wondering if this revolutionary view of our inner disposition is really true. You might confess that what you feel most deeply is actually an indifference toward God; perhaps while going through this lesson you've been trying to get in touch with more godly desires, but they seem to elude you.

Let me ask you a favor, as reflected in the next question.

14. Read Psalm 1 slowly (it's only six verses), seeking to quietly enjoy it. Then come back to this page.

Wasn't there something within you that stirred at the thought of becoming the tree mentioned in this Psalm? Didn't you find something deep within that was enticed by the prospect of "delighting" in God's Word and not just dutifully reading it? Write down here what impressed you:

15. Now let me ask you to do the same thing with Paul's prayer that begins in Ephesians 3:14. Read it slowly, quietly.

Again, wasn't there something deep within you that at least began to rise up in agreement with this prayer? Did the possibility of knowing "the love of Christ which passes knowledge" start to kindle an inclination at the core of your being for that very thing? Write down your thoughts:

A final question: What words of praise from someone else do you most long to hear? Can you imagine anything more thrilling than to hear Jesus tell you, "Well done, good and faithful servant.... Enter into the joy of your lord" (Matthew 25:21)? By comparison, I'm sure your regenerate heart counts any earthly praise as nothing but vain flattery.

And *that,* my friend, *comes only from your new disposition.*

OPTIONAL FURTHER STUDY (FOR GOING IN-DEPTH)—OUR NEW DISPOSITION

1. *Explore some of the following passages. How do they develop or reinforce or complement the doctrine of our new disposition as taught in this lesson? Record your thoughts.*

1 Kings 8:57-58; Psalms 51:10-12; 119:2,7,10-11,32-36,111-112; Proverbs 21:1; John 3:21,27; 6:45,65; 2 Corinthians 3:5; 5:14; Hebrews 13:20-21; James 1:16-18

2. *Look again at the classic New Covenant passages listed below. From what you've learned so far in this workbook, summarize in your own words the difference that the New Covenant makes in our disposition toward God and the things of God.*

   Jeremiah 31:33-34; 32:38-40; Ezekiel 11:19-20; 36:25-27

Both Faith and Feelings

The gladdest thing on earth is to have a real God.

R. A. TORREY

Tragically, too many Christians are almost wholly unaware of the new desires and disposition God has placed within them. We're told to "walk by faith and not by feelings." To avoid the mistake of living solely by emotions, we're encouraged just to do what is right, "and the feelings will follow."

All this is only partially true. The other side of the coin is that God has implanted within us a whole new set of desires, or "feelings," for us to make the most of. Emotions have been portrayed for too long as a hindrance to true godliness.

In this week's lesson we'll explore the emotional side of our faith and discipleship, as well as other practical ramifications of our new disposition in the Christian life. *(Remember to ask for the Holy Spirit's help in hearing and welcoming and obeying His words for you at this time.)*

1. How would you describe the role that your own emotions play in how you worship and obey God?

What About Emotions?

You may have figured out by now that I'm an admirer of Jonathan Edwards, who happens to be my fifth great-grandfather (which means I'm also related to Aaron Burr, one of American history's great scoundrels; you have to take the good with the bad!). What I admire most about Edwards isn't his intellect (perhaps unrivaled in American history), but his fervent passion and love for his Redeemer. Typical of passages in his *Personal Narrative* is this one: "The sense I had of divine things would often of a sudden kindle up, as it were, a sweet burning in my heart, an ardour of soul that I know not how to express."

One of the most significant works produced by this brilliant and passionate man of God is entitled *Religious Affections.* He wrote this book to correct an error in his day, one that many segments of today's evangelical church are facing as well. It's the dangerous misconception that emotions have little or no importance in true spirituality.

During the prosperous mid-eighteenth century in the New England colonies, most churches had settled into dead orthodoxy. Deep dependence on God was eroding. Bible truths were being taught, but often in a lifeless manner to congregations equally devoid of fervor.

The primary message from the pulpits was first, *Believe what is true,* and second, *Do what is right.* The combination of right beliefs and right behavior equaled true spirituality; emotions had little or nothing to do with it.

When God at this time used the ministry of Edwards to help bring about a revival known as the Great Awakening, it was opposed vigorously by many ministers and church leaders because of the emotional excesses and religious fanaticism it produced. Edwards responded to their criticism in *Religious Affections.*

He first distinguished between true and false religious affections. He acknowledged that some experiences were counterfeits in the flesh, but equally insisted that others were the result of God's Spirit.

Edwards also made the bold assertion that true Christian living consists "in great part" of true "holy affections." It isn't enough, he taught, to know and to do what is right; a Christian is also to "*experience* what is divine" on the level of the emotions and feelings. The Christian life, Edwards wrote, "contains things too great for us to be lukewarm." True Christianity "is *always a dynamic thing.* Its power is in the inward exercises of the heart."

Edwards's contention (which I believe is thoroughly biblical) is that, at a fundamental level, it's impossible *not* to live by feelings. Every decision we face, every action we're called on to take, is accompanied by a sense of either like or dislike—our affections, in other words. These affections, he explained, will motivate us either to accept and pursue that action or to oppose and turn away from it.

These affections or emotions can, of course, deceive and lead us astray; that's why God's revealed truth must always remain the final arbiter of what we do. But these same emotions can also help propel us toward greater godliness and devotion. The right approach isn't to demean or dismiss emotions altogether, but to utilize them fully in the purposes for which God gave them.

The true religious affections Edwards spoke of are in essence the new disposition God has given us through the New Covenant. If God has so mightily provided this new disposition for us, in all its emotional aspects, certainly He must want us to fully avail ourselves of it.

> "The first effect of the power of God in the heart in regeneration, is to give the heart a divine taste or sense...to cause it to have a relish of the loveliness and sweetness of the supreme excellency of the divine nature."
>
> —Jonathan Edwards

DUTY OR DESIRE?

Many times we approach the desire for God's will as either something we must work up or something that really doesn't matter so long as we *do* what's right. Certainly we should always do what's right, whether or not we feel so inclined. But God has seen to it that we're internally resourced with dependable, divinely implanted affections that make doing His will more of a spiritual outing than a spiritual chore.

2. How strongly do you sense your own desire to obey God's commands? Do you ever feel blocked in experiencing that desire? If so, what do you think might be causing this?

Think of it from God's point of view. Suppose I were to come home one day with a bouquet of the finest red roses for my wife, and after she thanked me I responded, "You're welcome, Sandy—I'm only doing my duty as your husband."

How would she feel? Not very warmed, I can assure you. When we come before God with our bouquet of dry, dutiful obedience, it's the same for Him.

It isn't just obedience God is after; it's a certain kind of obedience: "Serve the

> "They [the redeemed] have spiritual excellency and joy by a kind of participation of God. They are made excellent by a communication of God's excellency. The saint has spiritual joy and pleasure by a kind of effusion of God on the soul."
>
> —Jonathan Edwards

LORD with *gladness*" (Psalm 100:2). "These things I have spoken to you," Jesus said, "...that your *joy* may be full" (John 15:11).

3. Explore what some of these passages teach us about the emotions God wants us to have as part of our obedience. Summarize your findings.

    Deuteronomy 12:10-12; 28:47-48; Psalm 107:21-22; Acts 2:46-47; Galatians 5:22-23; Philippians 4:4

The kind of obedience that brings pleasure to God's heart and glory to God's name is the glad-hearted, voluntary offering of grace-soaked saints. It's a glad-heartedness that ultimately can come only from God Himself through His gift of our new disposition.

This is one of the most liberating truths I know of in Christianity. I spent so many years trying to muster up the desire for what I knew God was requiring of me, or praying that God would change my heart. The good news of sanctification is that *God has already changed* my heart, and yours as well. Our role now is to fall back in faith on the unalterable change God made within us at conversion—a disposition shot through with godly affections from the Holy Spirit.

> "God's aim is not to constrain men's submission by an act of raw authority; His aim is to ravish our affections with irresistible displays of His glory. The only submission that fully reflects the worth and glory of the King is glad submission. No gladness in the subject, no glory to the King."
>
> —John Piper

This God-intentioned desire is why the believer living in sin is really the most miserable creature on earth. He can't get the divine bent of his soul taken away, yet that bent robs him of the ability to fully enjoy sin. He can't escape knowing at the deepest level of his being that he was made for God, that his rebellion against righteousness is really kicking against the goads.

On the other hand, living as an outright disciple of Christ is the greatest favor a believer can do himself. When is an eagle most satisfied—in a cage or out in nature? Obviously out in nature, because eagles were created by God for such soaring freedom. Likewise no believer can be fully satisfied while caged in sin. Each of us was made to soar, to feel the currents of God's righteousness lifting us to ever-increasing heights of godliness.

UNRESTRAINED INDULGENCE

The New Covenant doesn't mean any kind of downgrade in obeying God. His commands are not suggestions, helpful hints, or practical advice; they're royal decrees, the King's rightful demands upon His subjects. To disregard or disobey them will always be high treason against heaven. But in the New Covenant, God has also provided a new, internal appetite for knowing and doing these same decrees.

God has turned the "have to's" into "want to's." He has caused His unwavering commands to become an inbred *delight* to our new nature.

I don't believe *delight* is too strong a word to describe the depth of pleasure our new disposition holds for God's standards. For every command He gives, He has infused within us a vigorous, holy inclination toward keeping it.

This is why Jesus said, "My food is to do the will of Him who sent Me, and to finish His work" (John 4:34). He knew that doing God's will brought strength and vigor to His soul, which is always the case when divine disposition connects with divine will.

4. Study Romans 7:21-25. What does this key passage teach us about our new disposition—as well as about the old one? Summarize your findings.

As Paul depicted his own struggle between obedience and sin, He described himself as "one who wills [literally "desires"] to do good" (Romans 7:21). He saw himself as someone who fundamentally wanted to do God's will. In his "inward man," Paul insisted, "I delight in the law of God" (Romans 7:22). The Greek word here for "delight" is quite strong; from its root we derive our word *hedonism.* And what is this "inward man" Paul spoke of? It's the new Paul, the real Paul.

That, my friend, is the new you as well. Your essential identity is that of desiring to do God's will. You can't help it; that's how God rewired you at your new birth. At the deepest core of our being, you and I "delight in the law of God." Our inner man and the law of God are never at odds; rather, our new disposition hedonistically enjoys the deep and holy pleasure of being united with God and His ways.

5. In light of what you've learned in this workbook, where in your own experience have you found that your deepest desire truly is to do God's will—that you actually delight to obey Him?

That's why *true obedience is the unrestrained indulgence of our new nature.* Obedience to God isn't just denying our flesh, though that will always be involved. It's also satisfying our new, divinely bestowed appetite for godliness. God calls us to a life of shamelessly glutting this new nature with the delicacies of Spirit-wrought obedience.

This is why James described the Word of God as "the law of liberty." God's commands are designed not to enslave us, but to free us to experience what we were redeemed for. "He who looks into the perfect law of liberty and continues in it, and is not a forgetful hearer but a doer of the work, *this one will be blessed in what he does* [literally, "in the doing"]" (James 1:25). The word here for "blessed" speaks of an interior, supernatural joy. It's the joy of glutting our new nature.

SPIRITUAL CONNECTORS FOR SPIRITUAL INDULGENCE

There's nothing in the New Covenant that validates or encourages us to neglect what are commonly referred to as "spiritual disciplines"—such things as prayer, fasting, Bible study, and Scripture memorization. "*Exercise yourself* toward godliness," Paul commanded Timothy (1 Timothy 4:7), and we need that exercise as well. There's no inherent legalism whatsoever in doing these things.

I prefer the term "spiritual connectors" for these practices, because they're necessary for connecting us with the presence of God in spiritually enriching ways. Each one is indeed a discipline in the sense that our flesh always opposes them, but each is meant also to satisfy the deepest hunger of our new disposition—for knowing God in all His ravishing fullness. *Every spiritual discipline is at the same time a spiritual indulgence.* Through these spiritual connectors, God is calling us to satiate our souls with the only commodity that can fully satisfy them.

That's why when these things are done mechanically or to impress others or to obligate God to bless us, they lose all meaning. They become nothing more than "should's." But praying, studying, meditating, and memorizing will always be "want to's" when we exercise them with a view to God's glory, in dependence on His Spirit, and for the delight of knowing Him more intimately.

6. What spiritual disciplines or "connectors" have you found yourself enjoying most? Which have helped you the most?

7. How would you summarize your overall understanding and experience of spiritual disciplines—our "spiritual connectors" to God? What do you think it would mean for you to exercise them with more of a view to God's glory, in more dependence on His Spirit, and with more delight in His intimacy?

ENJOYING GOD'S WORD, PRAYER, AND WITNESSING

Does a newborn infant need a commandment to long for his mother's milk? Hardly. And this is the very image Peter gives of our partaking of Scripture—"As newborn babes, desire the pure milk of the word" (1 Peter 2:2). It's a command simply to do what is instinctive to us. We're to feast regularly on the Word of God for the same reason we eat—because we want to! God has placed an appetite within our hearts that cannot be satisfied with anything less than the bread, meat, and honey of God's Word.

The same is true for prayer. When Paul commands us to pray "in the Spirit," "with all perseverance and supplication" (Ephesians 6:18), he's telling us to merely cooperate with what the Spirit within us is already doing and has made us want to do. Prayer is the essential way we eagerly accept Scripture's warm invitation to "draw near" to God (Hebrews 10:22). Prayer's purpose, Oswald Chambers said, "is that we get ahold of God, not of the answer." "Prayer," wrote R. A. Torrey, "makes God real." "True prayer," wrote Samuel Zwemer, "is God the Holy Spirit talking to God the Father in the name of God the Son, and the believer's heart is the prayer room."

Present also within us is an inherent desire for evangelism. Scary as sharing our faith can be, it's the innate yearning of our new heart. We were born to reproduce. There's an incomparable depth of joy and exhilaration of spirit awaiting every believer in the high adventure of warring on behalf of God's kingdom. Charles Spurgeon identified a "perfect, overflowing, unutterable happiness of the purest and most ennobling order" that he had never known before helping others find the Savior.

The good news about our new disposition is one of the most joyous and liberating truths in Christianity; it's also one of the best hidden. I've no doubt Satan wants to keep it this way because of the tremendous damage it would do to his kingdom. When God's people reach deep within and realize that evangelism is something they *want* to do, not just *should* do, the impact may be staggering.

"Even if I were utterly selfish and had no care for anything but my own happiness, I would choose, if I might, under God, to be a soul-winner; for never did I know perfect, overflowing, unutterable happiness of the purest and most ennobling order till I first heard of one who sought and found the Saviour through my means. No young mother so rejoiced over her firstborn child, no warrior was so exultant over a hard-won victory."

—Charles Spurgeon

SEEING OTHERS REALISTICALLY

8. Meditate on 2 Corinthians 5:14-17. How are we now enabled in Christ to view other believers?

Because of the New Covenant we can say with Paul, "From now on, we regard no one according to the flesh" (2 Corinthians 5:16). Instead we can view all other believers with this radical assumption: *They desire to do the will of God.*

In the New Testament, no group of believers showed less tangible evidence of being newly created in Christ than those in Corinth. Yet Paul affirmed to them that the Spirit of God had engraved God's law upon their hearts, and with clear confidence he wrote more about New Covenant realities to them than to any other church. Where did this confidence come from? "Through Christ toward God" (2 Corinthians 3:4), he said. Paul knew the Corinthians were participants in the New Covenant, not primarily because of visible fruit in their lives, but because of the certainty of Christ's abiding work in their hearts.

If our children are believers, we can have the same confidence about them. Deep down they want to do the will of God, hard as this is to believe sometimes. We need to continually affirm the reality of their new disposition along with any correction of their fleshly living. We can do this with statements such as "I know you really want to be a person of integrity" or through asking questions that speak to their new heart, such as "What do you really want?" or "Did that feel good deep down?"

The Old Covenant approach to all these things is to emphasize *only* the "should," then add the exhortation to "do what is right." The way of the New Covenant is to point out the "want to" along with the "should," then emphasize the deep joy of glorifying God through doing what is right by the power of God.

This is why I no longer see preaching and teaching as an attempt to convict and challenge Christians to do what they have no real desire for. Instead my role is to cooperate with God in coaxing to the surface their deepest longing, while also exposing the foolishness and perversity of living contrary to their divine design.

9. As you relate to other believers around you, how might you rely more fully on the Lord's power in helping you remember that their deepest emotional reality is a fundamental desire for God? Record your analysis here.

OPTIONAL FURTHER STUDY (FOR GOING IN-DEPTH)—DESIRING GOD

1. *Read prayerfully through Psalms 63 and 84 (or another similar passage you may want to choose). Find the verses that are most meaningful to you as an emotional expression of your longing for God. Then record those thoughts here in your own words of prayer.*

2. *How do these passages deepen your understanding or experience of your new disposition?*
   Psalms 26; 37:4; 122:1; Isaiah 26:7-9; 58:13-14; Habakkuk 3:17-19; Matthew 5:4,6; 1 Peter 1:6-9

Releasing Your New Power

New Testament Christianity is not just a formal, polite, correct, and orthodox kind of faith and belief. No! What characterizes it is this element of love and passion, this pneumatic element, this life, this vigour, this abandon, this exuberance.

D. MARTYN LLOYD-JONES

May I confess a fantasy of mine? I've always wanted to fly. Without an airplane, that is. I know it's neurotic, but I can't help it. I've even had dreams where I was floating, even soaring, just using my own two arms. It was great, and waking up was a disappointment.

But no matter how much I might like to fly there's obviously no way it's going to happen. My "want to" isn't connected with the resources necessary to make flying a "can do." My only hope is that there really are wings for us in heaven.

In the same way, it isn't enough simply to *want* to do God's will. Our best intentions and highest resolves are still impotent to overcome our flesh's downward pull.

To put it another way:

> New Purity + New Identity + New Disposition
> = frustration and defeat

Only when the provision of *New Power* is added to the equation does genuine victory become possible.

In this lesson we'll behold the liberating truth that God gives us not only a new set of "want to's" for doing His will, but also a new "can do" through His Spirit to actually carry out our new inclinations.

TELL THEM 'OW

1. According to what Jesus says in John 5:39-40 and what Paul says in Galatians 3:21, what is it that the Scriptures themselves cannot provide or produce?

2. How would you explain what Paul meant when he said in 2 Corinthians 3:6, "The letter kills, but the Spirit gives life"?

"The ministry of the New Covenant has its glory and its fruit in this, that it is all to be a demonstration of the Spirit and of power."

—Andrew Murray

3. What do you learn about our innate inability to do good from God's words in Jeremiah 13:23, and Jesus' words in John 6:63?

Scottish philosopher Thomas Carlyle was once sitting around the family fire, chatting with his parents about church and preachers. "Well, I will tell you one thing," he boldly asserted. "If I were ever to preach, I'd make short work of it. I would go up to the pulpit, look out on the congregation, and tell them this: 'You good people know what you should be doing. Now go home and do it!'"

After a pause, Carlyle's mother, a godly saint, looked him in the eyes and responded, "Aye, Thomas, but would ye tell them 'ow? Would ye tell them 'ow?"

Isn't this the great question facing each of us? Not *what* we should be doing, but *how* to do it. How do we find the power to carry out what God has made us want to do through our new disposition?

God has given us the answer through the New Covenant: "I will put My Spirit within you and cause you to walk in My statutes" (Ezekiel 36:27). God gives us a new "can do" through His Spirit to carry out the new "want to's" of our new disposition. Only *God* can fulfill through us what *God* has motivated within us.

This new power from God's Spirit is the same power that raised Christ from the dead. It is also the new power that *alone* can resurrect us from the defeated, deathlike quality of life to which our flesh seeks to hold us in bondage.

4. In what areas of life do you most quickly feel the need for God's promised power?

Skis, But No Boat

5. Two words are used at the end of Hebrews 7:18 to describe the law. What are they, and what does each one mean?

No matter how much we *want* to obey them, God's standards for us as outlined in His Word can never *in themselves* infuse life-giving power. In fact, they actually breed death in the flesh. As we've seen, law agitates the flesh, stimulates sin, provokes guilt, and thunders forth condemnation—in short, "the letter kills," as Paul said (2 Corinthians 3:6). I've found in my own life that when I view obedience to one of God's commands only as a "should," an internal resistance and deadness toward that very command tends to set in immediately.

Only resurrection power can lift this burden and provide the rest of soul Jesus promises. And this life-giving power is found only in a Person, not in precepts. "The letter kills, but the Spirit gives life" (2 Corinthians 3:6).

Whenever the "should's" of the Christian life become our central focus, we revert to living under a code (the letter) rather than through a Person (the Spirit). When we feel the legitimate command of God hammering down apart from supernatural provision, we droop under such unbearable weight.

6. Can you relate to this? In what ways have you ever experienced the weary discouragement of focusing too much on the "should's" of the Christian life, instead of living by the Spirit's power?

It's like being in a lake with water skis but with no motorboat. The skis offer direction and stability (as the law does), but they cannot, of themselves, keep you skimming over the waters. They can't even keep you from sinking.

Only Christ's resurrection power, the new power of the New Covenant, can keep us from sinking into the dark waters of deathlike living, so that we instead arise and move forward in the glorious adventure of supernatural living.

7. Study some of the following passages. If they're familiar to you, ask the Holy Spirit to help you view them in a fresh way. What do you learn from them about the new power available to us as believers?

   John 14:12-14; Acts 1:8; Romans 6:4-6; 8:10-11; 14:17;
   1 Corinthians 15:57-58; Philippians 3:10-11; Colossians 1:28-29

WANTING A PIECE OF THE ACTION

What keeps us from supernaturally moving forward more often?

You'll recall our earlier "what-why-how" requirements for something to qualify as good from God's perspective: It must be done *in accordance with the standard of God, for the glory of God,* and *through the Spirit of God.*

We have no chance of ever accomplishing such requirements *in our natural state.* This is why Paul admonished the Galatians, "Are you so foolish? Having begun in the Spirit, are you now being made perfect by the flesh?" (Galatians 3:3).

To think our spiritual growth can be empowered by that which is innately hostile to God—our flesh—is not only wrong, it's lunacy.

Yet it's so hard to yield fully to this truth. Our flesh desperately wants in on the action. It yearns to get at least partial credit for the good in our lives. It strives for at least some control and violently protests the terrifying prospect of relying only on God.

You see, our problem isn't in *trusting* God; it's in trusting God *alone*. We want to know His help is there when we've run out of options, but our flesh can't bear the thought of His being our only option.

8. In what ways have you seen this tendency in your own life of not wanting to trust in God alone—of depending upon anything in your life other than the Holy Spirit's power?

A WALKING CIVIL WAR

9. Turn again to Romans 7, and look in a fresh way at verses 14-25. In your own words, how would you explain Paul's spiritual experience as he described it in this passage?

10. How would you summarize the core struggle Paul was facing?

11. In what ways do you find yourself able to relate personally to what Paul said here?

12. What did Paul have to become convinced of before he could move on to the realities he taught in Romans 8:1-4? (See especially 7:18,24-25.)

In this portion of Paul's letter to the Romans, we find him caught in the throes of wanting to live for God but being dragged away by the power of his flesh. "For what I am doing, I do not understand. For what I will to do, that I do not practice; but what I hate, that I do" (Romans 7:15).

Paul was a walking civil war, caught between the pull of his flesh and the tug of his new nature. Words like *frustrated, overwhelmed, hopeless, restless,* and *guilt-ridden* are all a fair description of his Christian experience here—and perhaps they describe your Christian experience now as well.

Is this the normal Christian life? The answer is both yes and no.

The answer is yes in that all this is clearly normative. There will never come a time when you and I are not a walking civil war to some degree. "For the flesh lusts against the Spirit, and the Spirit against the flesh; and these are contrary to one another, so that you do not do the things that you wish" (Galatians 5:17). Until heaven, our battle against the flesh will never cease.

In another sense the answer is an emphatic no. God never intended His children to resign themselves to spiritual defeat as a way of life. "Thanks be to God who always leads us in triumph *in Christ*" (2 Corinthians 2:14). God, who provided His Son to remove the penalty of our sins, also provides His Son to defeat the pressing power of our sins. While the reality of our war with sin will never cease, the intensity of that battle is dramatically affected by how fully we appropriate the provision of the New Covenant, especially our new power.

We access this power of Christ through the Holy Spirit within. Therefore Paul exhorts us, "Walk in the Spirit, and you shall not fulfill the lust of the flesh" (Galatians 5:16). He didn't say that by walking in the Spirit we wouldn't *experience* the lust of the flesh; rather, we won't fulfill those lusts if we rely on the Spirit's resurrection power.

But until we become convinced to the core of our being that only Christ Himself provides the power for godliness, we'll continue to thwart His ministry within us by unwittingly depending on our flesh.

Embracing Inadequacy

Because my father died when I was young, there were many things I never learned growing up, including basic tasks like house repairs and car maintenance.

One of the most important skills I failed to pick up was leadership. As a result, I've spent most of my life running from it. Frankly, I find leadership—whether at home or church—to be scary. A part of me would love to always follow and let someone else take the risks. But God hasn't seen fit to allow this. For whatever reason, He's placed me in many situations requiring me to lead.

What has helped me in leadership more than anything else has been learning to embrace my inadequacy. (It's one thing to admit inadequacy; it's a very different thing to embrace it.) When a difficult decision must be made or a hard situation handled, I'm helped most by going before the Lord and saying something like…

"Lord, I don't have a clue what to do here. I'm fearful and would love to not be in this situation. Heaven looks really good now, and this would be a great time for You to come back.

"But if that can't be, then I need You to take me through this every step of the way. I have nothing to offer of my own ingenuity or strength; I need Your wisdom and power as badly as I need the air I breathe.

"As I move forward, help me do so with desperate dependence upon You every second. I joyously and unreservedly confess that I'm not a leader, I'm not able to handle this situation on my own, and any good must come solely through You. I simply ask You now to flow through me, Lord Jesus, and help me stay out of Your way."

Unless I begin by embracing my inadequacy in this way, I end up either leading in my flesh or backing away altogether.

13. In what ways is God helping you learn to fully embrace your inadequacy so that you can fully rely on the new power that is His gift to you? How would you describe what you've learned personally in this regard?

WHO, NOT WHAT

Another word to describe this embracing of inadequacy is *brokenness.* What I mean by brokenness isn't primarily anguish of heart (though that may be there), but absence of self-confidence. It's tossing overboard any hope of producing anything good on our own. Until Paul could say with heartfelt conviction, "For I know that in me (that is, in my flesh) *nothing good dwells*" (Romans 7:18), he remained too strong for God to be able to help.

We must come to the absolute end of our spiritual rope. As long as we call out, "O weak man that I am, I need help to make it," we're still too strong for God's power to fully intervene in our lives. We'll be ready for Christ to start moving us forward toward victory only when we cry out in despair, as Paul did: "O wretched man that I am! Who will deliver me from this body of death?" (Romans 7:24).

That means turning for help in the right direction, as Paul did, and not reaching for a counterfeit rope that can't do the job. Paul didn't ask, "*What* will deliver me?" but "*Who* will deliver me?" He then gave the answer: "I thank God—through *Jesus Christ our Lord!*" (Romans 7:25). Only the indwelling Christ can overcome the downward pull of sin's power in our flesh.

Tragically, most sanctification systems pursued by Christians today are based on a "what"—spiritual disciplines, counseling, Christian service, and so on. These can be helpful in leading us to the "Who," but they're impotent in themselves to deliver us from sin's power.

Until we ruthlessly shed all hope and confidence in our own ability to carry out God's will, no amount of sound Bible teaching on the subject will make any prac-

"Brokenness is the admission that the flesh is utterly insufficient
for the job it has taken on."

—Larry Crabb

tical difference in our lives. That's why many of us need a kind of reconversion in which we come to Christ for sanctification with the same desperate dependence we had when we came to Him for salvation. Or in the words of Paul, "*As* you therefore have received Christ Jesus the Lord, *so walk in Him*" (Colossians 2:6). Continue just the way you began—utterly needy, radically dependent.

14. Record here your reactions and questions after reading the previous paragraph. Are you in any need of such a "reconversion"?

AN IMPORTANT BALANCE

Continuing in Christ in this way will mean maintaining an important balance that often is neglected.

If we focus only on our new provisions through the New Covenant without properly taking into account our fallen, earthly nature, unwarranted optimism will result. We'll fail to appropriately recognize our human depravity and the inescapable reality of struggle.

But if we focus only on our fallen nature without properly taking into account our new provisions, it will cause unwarranted resignation. We'll fail to utilize our divine resources and remain stuck at a needlessly low level of spirituality.

15. Which tendency would you say is more common in your own life—to fail to take into account your fallen nature, or to fail to take into account your new provisions?

The great present hope for the believer is something Paul reminds us of when he says that God is "working continuously in you so that you both *desire* and *do* the Father's good pleasure" (Philippians 2:13, author's translation). This assertion points to both our new disposition and our new power. There's never a time when God provides the power to do His will without also providing the desire; nor does He ever provide the desire without the power. God provides supernaturally both the yearning to do His will and the ability to accomplish it, but we must appropriate both by faith.

EMPOWERMENT FOR IMPACT

16. In Romans 15:18, how did Paul articulate the basis for judging success in ministry?

As we draw upon this new power, in radical dependence on the Holy Spirit's presence, what will it mean for us?

Among other things, it will enable us to reflect His Son to others and to advance His kingdom purposes in this world. Jesus foretold what His disciples would become through the Holy Spirit's power: "You shall be witnesses to Me...to the end of the earth" (Acts 1:8). He calls His followers to make converts and to present these converts "complete in Christ" (Colossians 1:28, NASB). *Christ is calling you and me and every believer to a life that furthers the gospel's worldwide penetration* as well as in-depth cultivation of that gospel in those who respond.

Does that seem impossible? It should. Mark this: *God will never call you to something you can do.* Period. If you can do what God has called you to *without* the new power God alone provides...*then you missed what God has called you to.* God calls us only to that which requires Him.

This is why Paul exclaimed with genuine humility in Romans 15:18 that he dared not speak of anything except what Christ had accomplished through him. Reliance on Christ was the secret behind Paul's impact on the world of his day; it's also the secret behind *our* impact on the world of our day.

17. What is it that God has specifically called you to in your life that can be fulfilled only by Himself?

ENLIGHTENMENT

18. How would you describe the Holy Spirit's ministry of enlightenment as taught in these passages?
   John 15:26; 16:13-15; 1 Corinthians 2:9-13; 2 Corinthians 3:14-18; 1 John 4:13

> "No good work is done anywhere without aid from the Father of lights."
>
> —C. S. Lewis

Dependence on God is also critical for opening us to the Spirit's ministry of inward enlightening. This is a God-wrought illumination that enables us to understand spiritual truth beyond a merely intellectual level. D. L. Moody used to say that the Bible without the Holy Spirit is like "a sundial by moonlight." It takes God's Spirit to spiritually comprehend the words He Himself authored. That's why it's so important for us to read God's Word in childlike dependence on the Spirit, permeating our reading and meditation with prayer.

19. How might you better appropriate the Holy Spirit's enlightenment of the Scriptures?

The Spirit also enlightens us to the excellencies and beauty of Christ. He takes the Lord's radiant realities and reveals them to our hearts with supernatural vividness so that we actually see "the light of the knowledge of the glory of God in the face of Jesus Christ" (2 Corinthians 4:6).

20. How might you better experience the Holy Spirit's enlightenment concerning the beauty and excellencies of Christ?

The Spirit of God also enlightens us concerning sins in our life. Ultimately all sin occurs because of a breakdown in our relationship with Christ. Whenever an act of sin is present in our life, deep reliance on Christ is absent. The Holy Spirit loves us too much and is too jealous for God's glory to allow such sin to go unexposed. He may convict us through other people, through His Word, or simply through His own quiet, piercing work in our souls.

In the apostle John's terminology, sin takes place only when "abiding" stops: "Whoever abides in Him does not sin" (1 John 3:6). Whatever *abiding* means (we'll explore it more later), it's such a profoundly powerful undertaking that it's impossible to be genuinely engaged in it and be sinning at the same time.

21. How might you rely more fully on the Holy Spirit's enlightenment concerning sin in your life?

OPTIONAL FURTHER STUDY (FOR GOING IN-DEPTH)—OUR NEW POWER

1. *Study carefully and thoroughly Galatians 5:16-25. How would you summarize what this passage teaches us about our new power, about our old and new dispositions, the work and power of the Holy Spirit within us, and our appropriate response to all these truths?*

> "Men are dependent on the power of God for every exercise of grace."
>
> —Jonathan Edwards

2. *Study also Romans 8. Ask God to help you look at this familiar chapter in a fresh way through the enlightenment of the Holy Spirit. How does this passage show the provisions of our new purity, our new identity, our new disposition, and our new power working together?*

Dynamic
Dependence

The Spirit is an imperative necessity.
Only the Eternal Spirit can do eternal deeds.

A. W. TOZER

Let me ask you a hard question, the answer to which has everything to do with understanding the vital significance of our new power.

Here it is:

1. If you had to choose between having Jesus at your side or the Holy Spirit in your heart, which would you choose?

Think about it: Christ physically at your side, actually telling you what to do and showing you how, or the Holy Spirit, invisibly, mystically residing within the deep recesses of your heart. Any way you slice it, it's not an easy choice.

The reality is that Christ has already made the choice for you. It's found in His words to His disciples: "It is to your advantage that I go away; for if I do not go away, the Helper [the Holy Spirit] will not come to you; but if I depart, I will send Him to you" (John 16:7). Why would Christ say that His own exit and the Holy Spirit's entrance would be to our advantage?

Imagine taking basketball lessons from Michael Jordan. He demonstrates exactly how to shoot, dunk, dribble, and steal. He patiently instructs you on all the game's intricacies. With all that great training and modeling, would you be able to play basketball like MJ? Obviously not.

But suppose there was a way Michael could mystically assimilate himself inside you so that your body became his suit of clothes. He could leap through you, shoot through you, dunk through you. It would no longer be you playing basketball, but Jordan playing through you.

Sound familiar? "It is no longer I who live, but Christ lives in me" (Galatians 2:20). The normal Christian life is not our living for Christ, but Christ's living through us. Our body becomes His suit of clothes so that He loves through us, worships through us, witnesses through us, prays through us, and flows through us purely and powerfully. He does this through the Spirit, whom Jesus portrayed as "rivers [literally, "floods"] of living water" flowing from the heart of everyone believing in Him (John 7:38). The indwelling Spirit of God produces the outflowing life that God requires of us.

How then do we go about opening the floodgates of our lives so these rivers can spill forth unhindered?

In this lesson we want to answer that question as we explore how to *appropriate* our new power through the Holy Spirit.

> "The redeemed are in every thing directly, immediately, and entirely dependent on God: they are dependent on Him for all, and are dependent on Him in every way."
>
> —Jonathan Edwards

A PICTURE TO THINK ABOUT

2. Take some time to meditate on Christ's familiar words in John 15:1-8. Ask for the Holy Spirit's enlightenment to see Jesus' illustration with new eyes.

(a) How would you summarize in your own words the most important truths the Lord wants us to learn from these words?

(b) Why would you say these truths are so important for maintaining a close relationship with Christ?

(c) In what significant ways do you see that this passage truly illustrates your own experience of Christ within? How would you describe what it means to actually do what Jesus talks about here—to "abide" (or "remain") in Him?

(d) How do you view this passage differently in light of the discoveries you've made while going through *Experiencing Christ Within*?

This picture Christ gave in John 15 of the vine and its fruit-producing branches is perhaps the most instructive passage in Scripture for appropriating our new power.

> *Only one life, 'twill soon be past;*
> *Only what's done through Christ will last.*

"Abide in Me, and I in you," Jesus said as He gave the picture. "Without Me you can do nothing."

The vine, He says, is Himself, and we're the branches. But what exactly is it that we can't do without Him?

Jesus gives the answer: "Bear fruit." Without abiding in Him, we cannot fulfill the very design for which we were created. There are, of course, many things we can blatantly do without Christ, as well as many that we can do *for* Christ but in the flesh. Anything of lasting value, however, can only be done *through* Christ, by abiding in Him.

Clearly, abiding is something more than just believing. But nowhere in Scripture does God give us a detailed analysis of the various components of abiding. If He did, I'm certain we would turn it into a formula rather than leaving it as it is— a pathway to vital relationship.

Instead, the Lord directs our attention to a vine with branches and tells us to meditate on the deeper spiritual realities conveyed by it, then commands us to go and do likewise. "I am the vine, you are the branches."

For our life in Christ, let me suggest three significant lessons to learn from the branch abiding in the vine.

CLOSE CONNECTION

A vine and its branch know no distance from each other; they're tightly connected, with no gaps. In the same manner, we're to maintain a close connection with the Lord, closing any known gaps in our relationship.

Unconfessed sin can create such a gap. If keeping our pride intact is more valuable than enjoying God's presence, we'll refuse to confess our sin honestly and humbly.

An unforgiving spirit can bring about a gap. Jesus said, "If you do not forgive men their trespasses, neither will your Father forgive your trespasses" (Matthew

6:15). These words have nothing to do with our eternal salvation but everything to do with our present experience of God.

Gaps in that experience result also from our having knowingly offended another believer without seeking to make it right. "Leave your gift there before the altar," Jesus says to anyone conscious of an unreconciled relationship yet seeking to approach God. "Go your way. First be reconciled to your brother, and then come and offer your gift" (Matthew 5:23-24). This doesn't mean every brother or sister will be willing to reconcile, but we'll have done our part. The gap between the Lord and us will be closed.

Besides closing such gaps, Jesus alludes to two primary ways for strengthening our connection with Him: "If you abide in Me, and *My words* abide in you, you will *ask* what you desire" (John 15:7). Prayer and immersing ourselves in God's Word are both intensely relational. Both are meant to lead us ever deeper into the Lord's presence; both are absolute musts for genuine abiding.

3. What are the possible gaps that may need closing in your own intimacy with the Lord? In what ways might God be prompting you to strengthen your connection with Christ?

DRAWING LIFE

The branch is continually and entirely dependent on the vine for vitality and support. Alone, it brings nothing to the fruit-bearing enterprise; all the good it accomplishes is drawn from the life-giving sap of the vine.

Jesus Himself lived the most dynamic life ever because He maintained the most dependent life ever. "The Son can do nothing of Himself," He declared (John 5:19). His example shouts from the mountaintops that we're as dependent on God for our spiritual life as we are on the air we breathe for our physical life.

JESUS: THE MOST DEPENDENT LIFE EVER

We see absolute dependence on God modeled most astonishingly in the life of our Lord. Listen closely to His words from John's gospel:

"Most assuredly, I say to you, the Son can do nothing of Himself, but what He sees the Father do; for whatever He does, the Son also does in like manner" (5:19).

"My Father has been working until now, and I have been working" (5:17).

"I can of Myself do nothing.... I do not seek My own will but the will of the Father who sent Me" (5:30).

"The Father who dwells in Me does the works" (14:10).

Jesus did nothing of His own initiative but joined in with what God was already doing. God the Father was always in the lead.

Jesus did nothing of His own invention. He was dependent upon His Father's example and sought only to mirror what He saw His Father doing.

Jesus did nothing of His own will. He didn't come to establish and fulfill His own ministry but the one designated for Him by the Father.

Jesus did nothing in His own strength. The ministry He unleashed upon the world was done wholly through the power of His indwelling Father.

What's the primary reason unbelievers don't come to Christ for salvation? They don't recognize their need. What's the primary reason believers don't come to Christ for sanctification? Exactly the same—we don't genuinely recognize our need.

"Apart from Me you can do *nothing*" (John 15:5, NASB)—those words have not a trace of exaggeration to them. Yet our flesh tries to keep the prideful hope alive of accomplishing something worthy on our own. Usually we try it in areas that we consider our strengths: our intellect, our personal discipline, our godly upbringing (if we were so blessed), our personality traits, or our Christian training or education.

4. Look up 1 John 2:6. In light of what you've learned about Christ's dependence on His Father, record here the fullest meaning you see in this passage.

5. In what ways could each of the following potentially draw us away from proper dependence on God?

(a) our intellect:

(b) our godly upbringing (if so blessed):

(c) our own personal discipline:

(d) our personality:

(e) our Christian ministry training:

The best intellect can never replace or even slightly lessen one's desperate need for the Holy Spirit's light. When we read our Bibles without bothering to ask for His enlightening, when we make plans and decisions without genuinely waiting to hear from God, we demonstrate our conviction that unaided intellect is all we need.

A genuinely Christian home can teach and show the way of life, but it does absolutely nothing for flesh improvement. It can train a child to be religiously refined and socially respectable, but that same child's flesh is still as utterly vile and allergic to true good as that of someone growing up on the streets. Our flesh may accommodate itself to whatever Christian culture it's been placed within, and it may never seek satisfaction through drugs or illicit sexuality, but not even a perfect upbringing can infuse it with such goodness that the Holy Spirit becomes any less essential.

Personal discipline or willpower originating from the flesh is typically rigid, relationally distant, and quietly smug in its own achievements. But self-control as a fruit of the Spirit is relaxed, is relationally enhancing, and humbly rejoices in what God has made possible.

Just as personal discipline can be a counterfeit of the self-control that is a fruit of the Spirit, so it is with any of our perceived personality strengths. Charm and empathy can be counterfeits for love, cheerfulness for joy, steadiness for peace. Obviously there's nothing wrong with personality—God grants one to all of us.

But it can subtly become our primary object of reliance in our relationships, leaving the Holy Spirit alone at the dance. Often what is called "leadership" in Christian circles is nothing more than a dominating personality.

Even Christian education and ministry training can draw us away from desperate dependence. It's very tempting to fall back on them rather than the Lord Himself. Christian training can provide helpful tools for ministry, but it can never provide strength for it.

Recently I was asked to meet with the parents of a college student who had just been killed. Before the meeting I kept asking myself, *What should I say in this situation?* There's nothing wrong with that question, but internally I was tense and insecure because I really had no answer. Subtly, I was seeking to fall back on ministry skills rather than on Christ Himself. My soul found no rest until I sensed the Lord assuring me that He would tell me what to say, but not until I got there. My primary responsibility was to love this mother and father out of my new heart, with the strength God would give me at that moment.

As it turned out the Lord didn't give me many words for them. But He did give me what I believe they needed most at the time: tears in my eyes and an arm around their shoulders.

A Divine Drunkenness

The branch remains fully open to the life of the vine flowing through it, quietly yielding to that which sustains its very existence. Only this produces fruit.

> "The spiritual leader...influences others not by the power of his own personality alone but by that personality irradiated, interpenetrated, and empowered by the Holy Spirit."
>
> —J. Oswald Sanders

6. We find another picture of this process in Ephesians 5:18. Record the two commands that are given here. Why do you think they're placed together like this?

What is Paul trying to illustrate through this seemingly offensive metaphor—a comparison between being filled with the Spirit and drunkenness?

Controlled might be the best word for it. When someone is drunk, he's being controlled by alcohol, dominated by something foreign to him. Consequently he does that which, when sober, he would never do. Being filled with the Spirit essentially means being yielded to a foreign influence—heaven's divine intoxicant, the Holy Spirit, who causes us to be inebriated with the Person of Christ and His glory so that we do things that are foreign to our natural being.

UPWARD, INWARD, OUTWARD

The Holy Spirit's ministry to us is *upward, inward,* and *outward.*

Upward—"Whoever drinks of the water that I shall give him will never thirst. But the water that I shall give him will become in him a fountain of water springing *up* into everlasting life" (John 4:14).

Inward—"that He would grant you, according to the riches of His glory, to be strengthened with might through His Spirit *in* the inner man" (Ephesians 3:16).

Outward—"He who believes in Me, as the Scripture has said, *out* of his heart will flow rivers of living water" (John 7:38).

This yieldedness to the Holy Spirit's control requires submission to His direction. Paul speaks of being "led by the Spirit" (Romans 8:14; Galatians 5:18). The Spirit is *on the move.* Our responsibility is to move with the movement.

Active Passivity

7. Look up Colossians 2:6. In light of what you've learned in this lesson about dynamic dependence on God, record here the fullest meaning you see in this passage. .

Appropriating our new power comes through what Francis Schaeffer aptly termed "active passivity." This, it seems to me, is exactly what abiding is all about. We have an active part to play. We're commanded to do something—abide. Yet, paradoxically, accompanying our activity there must be a passivity, a radical, diligent dependence.

Years ago, when I was a tennis instructor, a woman asked me to give lessons to her two sons. Needing the money, I gladly agreed, not bothering to ask their ages. The next day she brought her two sons, ages five and six. Each of them was holding an adult-sized racket. I could tell immediately we were in trouble.

After showing them how to grip and swing their rackets, I began tossing balls to them. Each in his turn completely missed the ball. By the time the boys were getting their rackets around, the ball had hit the backstop. We were going downhill in a hurry.

Then I asked a friend to toss the balls while I stood behind each boy, putting my hand over theirs as they gripped the racket. I told them to relax and I would hit the ball for them. As long as they relaxed in my strength, I was able to hit the ball over the net with them.

Then one boy said, "Okay, I can do it now." I stepped back and let him—and the results were disastrous. He asked if I would help him again, and I agreed. But this time, instead of fully relaxing in my strength and skill, he tried to help me. And as long as he was tensed up from trying to partially do it himself, I wasn't able to hit the ball over. He was too strong for me to work through him.

Finally he relaxed. Only then were we able to hit the ball again over the net. The secret? The little guy had to maintain close connection, desperate dependence, and utter yieldedness to me. He couldn't do it apart from me, nor could he do it by helping me; he merely cooperated with my working through Him. In a word, he was abiding.

The essence of abiding is that we fully cooperate with a Life not our own to bring forth fruit not our own. True godly character—"the fruit of the Spirit" (Galatians

---

"We are neither to think of ourselves as totally passive, as though God had stopped dealing with us as men, nor are we to think that we can do it ourselves. If we are to bring forth fruit in the Christian life, or rather if Christ is to bring forth this fruit by the agency of the Holy Spirit, there must be a constant act of faith, of thinking: *Upon the basis of Your promises I am looking for You to fulfill them.... Bring forth your fruit through me into this poor world.*

"That is what I mean by active passivity.... It is not that I disappear. However...I cannot do the Lord's work in my own energy, my own cleverness, my own persistence, 'charisma,' my own spiritual gifts and so on. I am there, but I must not count those things as the source of my power."

—Francis Schaeffer

5:22-23)—is the greatest evidence on earth of God's miracle-working power. God is most fully glorified through the ongoing radiance of a God-intoxicated life. And because of the presence of this new power in other believers' lives, I must view each one of them as a miracle awaiting greater unfolding.

8. (a) As we conclude this lesson, how do you think you can more fully tap into this new power in your own life?

(b) What are the possible gaps that may need closing in your own intimacy with the Lord?

(c) And how can you allow the reality of this new power to influence the way you view other believers?

OPTIONAL FURTHER STUDY (FOR GOING IN-DEPTH)—DEPENDENCE ON GOD

1. *How do these passages deepen your understanding or experience of dynamic dependence on God?*
   Psalms 22; 34; 46; 62; Isaiah 50:10-11; Luke 22:46; Acts 7:59; 2 Timothy 1:12; 1 Peter 2:21-23; 4:19

2. *What incidents from the life of Christ help you to see His total dependence on His Father in heaven? Record them here, along with relevant passages from the Gospels.*

The Adventure Continues

God's deepest purpose for the world is to fill it with reverberations
of His glory in the lives of a new humanity.

J O H N   P I P E R

As we more fully recognize and appropriate our new purity, our new identity, our new disposition, and our new power, we'll experience their divinely intended results—including new intimacy with God, new liberty in daily living, a new sense of community with other believers, and a new ministry through the Spirit.

In this lesson we want to think about these aspects of our lives from a deeper New Covenant perspective. We have time and space here to take only a brief glance at them, but my prayer is that for all the rest of your life you'll look differently at every aspect of your life and ministry as a result of the incredible New Covenant truths and provisions God has given you.

(Once more, remember to ask for the Holy Spirit's help in hearing and welcoming and obeying His words for you at this time.)

A Fresh Look at Our Intimacy with God

My boyhood idol was an Australian tennis great named Roy Emerson. Until Pete Sampras recently surpassed him, Emerson held the record for the most grand slam championships in tennis history. As someone whose life was dominated by tennis, I read everything I could about Emerson. I watched him on television and tried—not very successfully—to model my own tennis game after his. I knew all kinds of interesting tidbits about him. I would have given anything to meet him, but there was little chance.

All this changed in the spring of 1974. Through a strange set of circumstances, I was hired to work for Emerson at a tennis resort for several weeks. I still remember the thrill and nervousness of finally getting to meet him and the pleasure of discovering how warm-hearted, accepting, and encouraging he was in person.

In the following weeks I was privileged to spend a good amount of time with him. Besides working under him giving tennis lessons, I was with him often to eat, work out, and occasionally play golf. He invited me to play some exhibition tennis matches with him and really helped me with my game.

That broad grin I'd seen on his face in tennis magazines was even broader in person, especially when he pushed me beyond exhaustion. I'd often read about his feared backhand volley; now I discovered personally why it was revered.

Unexpectedly, he took a sincere interest in me, for which I'll always be grateful. He kindly answered my frequent questions about the places and events in the tennis world he had experienced.

It was all a dream come true beyond anything I could have imagined growing up.

I learned a very important lesson that spring. It's one thing to know *about* a person; it's a very different thing to come to know that individual personally.

"What fire is this that warms my soul?... O fire that burns forever, and never dies, kindle me! O light which shines eternally, and never darkens, illumine me!... How sweetly do you burn!"

—Augustine

TO FEEL THE FIRE

Nowhere is this more true than when it comes to knowing God.

How incomprehensible it is that God—the infinitely great God who is from everlasting to everlasting—passionately invites us not just to know about Him, but to know Him firsthand! He beckons us to gaze upon His excellence and beauty, to hear His voice, and to feel His touch within our souls. "He meant us to see Him," wrote A. W. Tozer, "and live with Him and draw our life from His smile."

It's one thing to know theological categories describing God's attributes; it's a very different thing to experience those attributes firsthand. Knowing God does involve an intellectual grasp of the truths of His being and His will, but it's much, much more. It's possible to gain a handle on the Word of God through diligent study and meticulous thought yet fail to significantly experience within our souls the fire of the Spirit of Him to whom the Scriptures point.

1. How would you explain the taste of Coca-Cola to those who've never tasted anything like it? What would you liken it to so that they could fully understand?

To answer that question adequately is probably impossible. To truly know its taste, they must drink it. To know God, we must taste Him. As an old Scottish saying puts it, "Some things are better felt than telt." Unless we know God's fiery presence in our souls, we can be scholars but never worshipers.

ALL FROM ABOVE

One of the most alluring promises in the New Covenant is this: "No more shall every man teach his neighbor, and every man his brother, saying, 'Know the LORD,' for *they all shall know Me,* from the least of them to the greatest of them, says the LORD" (Jeremiah 31:34).

Under the Old Covenant, God's people were called to "know the LORD" just as we are today. But only select individuals (normally prophets, priests, or kings) were granted significantly close access to God. Others had to go to a priest or elder for instruction—or to the written law itself. It always required an external source.

All this changes with the New Covenant. Every believer has as much access to God and His wisdom as any other believer. God isn't one iota more disposed to let Himself be known by Billy Graham than by you or me. His door is never closed to us while He meets with someone more important.

He delights to reveal His eternal wisdom to your seeking heart and His ravishing splendor to your soul. He does all this through the internal medium of His Holy Spirit (though external sources are often the instruments through which He works). God Himself does this for us because *it requires God to know God.* True spiritual understanding will never occur until it's given from above through the Holy Spirit.

"Blessed are you," Jesus once said to Peter, "for flesh and blood has not revealed this to you, but My Father who is in heaven" (Matthew 16:17). Subjects like science, mathematics, philosophy, and history require only "flesh and blood"—natural

"We pursue God because, and only because, He has first put an urge within us that spurs us to that pursuit."

—A. W. Tozer

human resources—to comprehend. Grasping the things pertaining to Christ, however, requires our Father in heaven revealing them to us, as He did to Peter. Through the New Covenant, this ongoing revelation is offered to all believers.

THE DANCE

God has placed within us, as part of our new disposition, a new upward passion, a restless yearning to worship Him.

To the Samaritan woman, Jesus pictured this passion of the Spirit as "a fountain of water springing up into everlasting life" (John 4:14). Elsewhere in the New Testament this word for "springing up" is translated "leaping." The tense of the word here denotes continual action. In other words, the Spirit of God within the regenerate heart of the believer is ceaselessly leaping toward heaven for communion with God and worship of the Father.

The Holy Spirit is never seen as passive in the Bible. He's always on the prowl, moving upward, moving outward. Our worship of God is to be carried out on the Spirit's coattails as He leaps incessantly toward the Father.

When we don't *feel* like this—when we think, *Forget the water springing up, just a trickle would be great*—the starting point for moving back toward God is to focus on the ceaseless exuberance of the Spirit within us. When what seems most real in our pursuit of God is apathy or dryness, has the Spirit lessened His leaping at all? No, a thousand times no. His passion for God never rides on our coattails. He keeps dancing whether or not we're at His side.

Normally (though not always), when our passion for God seems drained, it's because we've picked another partner to dance with. The Bible calls it idolatry; it's the sure drainpipe of godly passion.

The Spirit eagerly awaits us to rejoin Him in the dance (He "yearns jealously," as James 4:5 says). That's why repentance isn't working up a new desire or commitment to do right; it's turning a cold shoulder to those whom we've allowed to seduce us away from our original Partner and then rejoining Him in the dance of the ages. It's in His arms, with Him in the lead, that we can once again be swept up in divinely orchestrated communion and worship.

CHRISTIAN MYSTICISM

There's an undeniable mysticism to true Christian spirituality. The Spirit of God urges us upward to know and worship God the Father and God the Son, penetrating our inner being to spotlight and inflame spiritual realities.

This "Christian mysticism," Francis Schaeffer writes,

> is communion with Christ. It is Christ bringing forth fruit through me, the Christian.... There is to be experiential reality, moment by moment. And the glory of the experiential reality of the Christian, as opposed to the bare existential experience, or the religious experiences of the East, is that we can do it with all the intellectual doors and windows open. We do not need a dark room; we do not need to be under the influence of hallucinatory drugs; we do not need to be listening to a certain kind of music; we can know the reality of the supernatural here and now.

Without the Holy Spirit's illumination of these realities, we're like visitors in a darkened art museum. The portraits are just the same as when the lights were on; they didn't change by being plunged into darkness. But what a difference it makes to the beholder! He can know that great beauty lies directly in front of him, but he cannot view and admire that beauty—until the lights come back on.

This is why it takes more than the Bible to know God. It also requires the mystical, internal working of the Holy Spirit to make vital and dynamic today these words that He authored in the past.

Power's Reality

Let me ask two searching questions that I also ask myself:

2. If God were to withdraw His Spirit from this earth, how significantly would my spiritual life be altered? Would it come to a screeching halt, or continue on virtually unaffected?

3. What spiritual reality is there in my life that could not be duplicated by an unbeliever, no matter how hard they tried? What blatantly supernatural evidences of God leak through me?

God—who parted the Red Sea and raised His Son from the grave—this same God inhabits you and me. Our lives are designed to be a repeat performance of what happened at the Red Sea and at Christ's tomb. The miracles in our lives will be no less miraculous and no less dependent upon God's power for implementation. *The Christian life properly lived is an ongoing miracle*—a miracle empowered through truly knowing God.

A FRESH LOOK AT OUR FREEDOM IN CHRIST

The word *Christian,* writes Eugene Peterson,

> means different things to different people. To one person it means a
> stiff, uptight, inflexible way of life, colorless and unbending. To
> another it means a risky, surprise-filled venture, lived tiptoe at the
> edge of expectation.
>
> Either of these pictures can be supported with evidence…. But if
> we restrict ourselves to biblical evidence, only the second image can
> be supported: the image of the person living zestfully, exploring
> every experience—pain and joy, enigma and insight, fulfillment and
> frustration—as a dimension of human freedom, searching through
> each for sense and grace. If we get our information from the biblical
> material, there is no doubt that the Christian life is a dancing, leap-
> ing, daring life.

As believers we're called to stand fast in the freedom by which Christ has made
us free. Ours is to be "a dancing, leaping, daring life." But too many of us are stuck
in the religious mire of what has been termed "joyless moralism," holding tena-
ciously to moral duties but remaining disconnected from the explosive joy and freedom of the indwelling life of Christ.

One of God's intended results of the New Covenant is a Spirit-dependent
lifestyle of liberty. Anything less is slavery, either to the tyranny of law-based obedience or to the bondage of flesh-driven sensuality.

"A Christian is a perfectly free lord of all, subject to none. A Christian is a perfectly dutiful servant of all, subject to all."

—Martin Luther

"If the Son makes you free," Jesus promised, *"you shall be free indeed"* (John 8:36). May God grant us grace and courage to leave behind the fetters of legalism or license and to soar as the golden eagles He has made us, swept along in the currents of His Spirit to the glorious adventure of supernatural living, attaining a joy that the shallow, earthly imitation called "happiness" can never touch.

Only then will we be "free indeed."

AVOIDING EXTREMES

4. How would you explain and define "freedom in Christ" (or "Christian liberty") as this concept relates to your own everyday life?

What exactly is this thing called freedom, and how do we find and maintain it?

Whatever genuine Christian freedom is, it absolutely requires the presence and power of God's Spirit. "Where the Spirit of the Lord is, *there* is liberty," Paul said (2 Corinthians 3:17). The Spirit's presence will keep us alert to two opposing extremes that we want to avoid at all costs.

The first extreme is to be so concerned with the potential abuse of freedom that we pull in the reins and lose the legitimate and godly exuberance that is our birthright as God's children. Many preachers and teachers are more concerned with keeping their people morally in check than with freeing them for God's adventure of supernatural living. Yes, it's always wrong when freedom is abused, but freedom transforms and elevates a believer's walk with God to heights that stale rule keeping never can.

Reinhold Niebuhr has said it well:

> You may be able to compel people to maintain certain minimum standards by stressing duty, but the highest moral and spiritual achievements depend not upon a push but a pull. People must be charmed into righteousness.

This is why Paul wrote with white-hot ink, "Stand fast therefore in the liberty by which Christ has made us free, and do not be entangled again with a yoke of bondage" (Galatians 5:1).

The opposite extreme is using freedom as a ticket to fleshly indulgence. Paul also warned, "Do not use liberty as an opportunity for the flesh" (Galatians 5:13). Such misconstrued freedom results when preachers and teachers drain away God's holiness from His love. Our flesh can quickly translate freedom in Christ into license for self-centered and sin-justifying living. This is not true freedom, but only spiritualized and rationalized bondage.

PURPOSE-DRIVEN UNRESTRAINT

I like to define true freedom in Christ as *purpose-driven unrestraint.* It's a liberty that's possible only because, in the New Covenant, we have both the desire and the power to do God's will. We're free in the fullest sense only when those two things come together. Power without desire results in begrudging obedience at best. Desire without power results in frustrated intentions. When we have both power and desire, we have the freedom of being able to do what we most deeply want to do.

One popular Bible teacher has defined freedom as "not the right to do what we want, but the ability to do what we ought." Do you see the problem with this definition? It's only half the story. It assumes that our "want's" and God's "ought's" are always opposed to each other. The wondrous beauty of the New Covenant is that

God has made the "ought's" of His Word the "want's" of our regenerate heart, then flooded our inner beings with resurrection power so we can bring these to fruition. This is freedom indeed.

Then we can gladly "give in" to our divine design and say yes to God's goal for us, which is to glorify Him through Jesus Christ—"to be prisms refracting the light of God's glory into all of life," as John Piper says.

EXHILARATION

We do well to remember that the word *freedom* meant much more to the original readers of the New Testament than it does to us. Over half the population in the Roman world was enslaved. Aristotle's view was widely held: "A slave is a living tool, just as a tool is an inanimate slave."

To experience freedom, therefore, went beyond "being unbound"; it meant exhilaration—the dancing and leaping that Peterson spoke of.

Freedom in Christ is a spiritually intoxicating wine, a breathtaking flight into space, a soul-thrilling escape from enemy territory. It's the spiritual exhilaration of having one's soul set free for the high adventure of a God-enabled assault upon life.

THE RIGHT MASTER

Paradoxically, ultimate freedom also means being enslaved to the right master. Virtually every passage in the New Testament dealing with freedom contains immediate references to slavery as well. This shouldn't surprise us. In reality there's no such thing as absolute freedom; the only real freedom man has is the freedom to choose his master.

We're all enslaved, either to God or to sin and idols. We all go through life as driven people; the only question is whom we've chosen to put in the driver's seat. We may be comfort-driven, approval-driven, security-driven, achievement-driven, wealth-driven, fitness-driven, health-driven, ministry-driven, or Christ-driven. Never, ever, are *we* alone in control.

"Having been *set free* from sin," Paul tells believers, "you *became slaves* of righteousness" (Romans 6:18). As Christians, our experience of freedom continues only while we choose to stay within our new bondage to righteousness. There's no such thing as joint citizenship between righteousness and sin. We're no longer free to fully enjoy frolicking in sin, because the yearning for righteousness that's now deep within us always tags along to the party.

Being "free indeed," Jesus said, comes only when "*the Son* makes you free" (John 8:36). True freedom comes only by yielding to His authority, His presence, and His power. As we radically abandon ourselves to our rightful Master, we'll find ourselves in glad bondage, and our souls will sing for joy at coming home. That which was imposed upon us externally is now implanted within us supernaturally through His New Covenant provision of our new disposition and power.

I've found again and again in my own life how this truth helps me know whether I'm operating out of the flesh or the Spirit. There's always an inner tenseness when I'm trying to do the will of God out of my flesh. It's a heaviness within, a kind of grasping that never feels clean. When the Spirit is in control, there's an inner relaxation, a sense of something flowing that I'm not having to work at, a joyous boldness that feels dependently clean.

5. Read the sidebar on the next page entitled "Mature Freedom." In what ways are the perspectives of mature freedom not yet fully yours? In particular, how free are you to fully love those whom God has placed in your life?

A Fresh Look at Community

Francis Schaeffer points out that at the Fall, we humans disconnected not only from God, but also from ourselves and from others. The oneness that had flowed naturally and effortlessly between Adam and Eve was now shattered.

And yet we cannot shake free of our yearning as God's image-bearers for relationship with others. We must either divert it or deny it.

MATURE FREEDOM

Our freedom to truly love highlights what I like to call the difference between adolescent freedom and mature freedom.

Adolescent freedom asks only, What am I free *from?* Mature freedom asks also, What am I free *for?*

Adolescent freedom asks only, Is it forbidden? Mature freedom asks also, Is it helpful?

Adolescent freedom embraces the liberty "to do my own thing"; mature freedom embraces the liberty "to do Christ's thing."

Adolescent freedom often confuses legalism with obedience; mature freedom understands the difference.

Mature freedom knows not only the exhilaration of being free from the wrong master, but also the greater exhilaration of being enslaved to the right Master.

Mature freedom recognizes that one is both free and a servant to others, as Luther noted: A Christian is both "a perfectly free lord of all" and "a perfectly dutiful servant of all."

Mature freedom realizes not only freedom from others' opinions, but also concern for the "weak." Mature freedom enjoys liberty but feels no need to prove it.

Like all the connections we lost at the Fall, God-honoring unity and deeply satisfying community can begin to be restored only through our New Covenant provisions. In the New Covenant, God made this promise for His people: "I will give them one heart" (Jeremiah 32:39). The only solution for our inbred disconnectedness with one another is God's determined resolve—*"I will"*—and His grace—"I will *give."* God and God alone is the foundation and source for our new community.

Our truest bond is never based on our group or cause, our denomination or theological camp, the spiritual experiences we have in common, or the kind of ministry we're involved in—but always on our common Christ. He is the foundation of our common fellowship, made possible by a common death. We are indwelt by a common Spirit and designed for a common purpose.

This is why, as Dietrich Bonhoeffer wrote, "Christian brotherhood is not an ideal which we must realize; it is rather a reality created by God in Christ in which we may participate." Unity is not something to be achieved, but something to be kept intact. Paul tells us "to *keep* [not "achieve" or "produce"] the unity of the Spirit in the bond of peace" (Ephesians 4:3). You can "keep" only what was already present. And this harmony is "of the Spirit"; it's God-produced, not man-manufactured.

Genuine community can never take place where believers fail to appropriate and operate from supernatural resources. God has designed His new community so that its success requires Him. When His resources are neglected, the dryness in our hearts and the poverty of our own fleshly resources will cause relating with one another to degenerate into varying degrees of people-draining.

So often we approach unity from a fundamentally Old Covenant approach, frantically trying to make it happen and produce something we believe is fundamentally absent. But the unshakable reality is that *whenever* two believers meet, unity *is* present; the only question is whether it's being actualized.

THE DIFFERENCE IT MAKES

6. Why do you think God is so keenly interested that His children be well connected and dynamically united? Answer as fully as you can.

The answer we usually think of first to the above question is that our unity will help strengthen and encourage one another toward greater godliness. We view community primarily as a laboratory for our Christian development.

But God sees our community primarily as an exhibition, not a laboratory. Our Spirit-drenched oneness is the most important way His spectacularness is displayed on earth.

In the first centuries of the church, the supernatural concern and oneness among believers rocked the world back on its heels. "It is incredible to see the fervor with which the people of that religion help each other in their wants," wrote the second-century writer Lucian. "Their first legislator [Jesus] has put it into their heads that they are brethren."

In our relationships with each other, there's more at stake than simply enjoying one another's company, wonderful as that can be. God has designed for public display a network of diverse individuals whose lives are to be so beautifully interconnected that it's nothing short of stunning. The name of this network is the *church,* God's "called out ones." Our specialty is to be a relational excellence that unmistakably reflects the love within and between the Trinity. Never does the world see Christ more clearly than when His love flows freely among believers.

7. Look closely at Romans 15:5-7. In this passage, how do you see our unity portrayed, what purpose is expressed for our unity, and what instruction are we given for maintaining that unity? Record your findings here:

Notice what was in the heart of Jesus as He prayed for you and me and our brothers and sisters: "that they may all be one, as You, Father, are in Me, and I in You; that they also may be one in Us, *that the world may believe that You sent Me*" (John 17:21). Our unity, Francis Schaeffer says, is our "final apologetic." By this, more than anything else, non-Christians will pass judgment on whether or not Christianity is true.

The vast majority of people whom I've seen trust Christ over the years didn't do so through a one-shot message or gospel presentation. Most of them began their pilgrimage toward Christ by hanging around the fringes of a group of believers. They became intrigued with how these believers cared for one another. Their curiosity was aroused; they had never seen anything like it. Their eventual coming to Christ is a direct answer to Christ's high priestly prayer two thousand years ago.

When it's all said and done, the song is right—they'll know we are Christians by our love.

GENERATING HEAT

As the highest purpose for our community, God's glory embraces many other purposes as well. For our sakes as well as His own, God has given us other members of the body to benefit from. Together we're commanded to "consider one another in order to stir up love and good works, not forsaking the assembling of ourselves together, as is the manner of some, but exhorting one another" (Hebrews 10:24-25). The word used in this passage for "stir up" means "to incite, stimulate, create a fever." Our community is to generate an internal heat that excites each one of us toward God-honoring living.

True fellowship differs from mere human friendship in the role that the supernatural plays. True fellowship moves believers closer to God as well as to one another. Do you know someone in whose presence you often feel your heart for God kindled? When was the last time you finished a conversation with another believer and left thinking, "I want to know Christ more deeply," or "I want to step out and risk what I know God is calling me to"? I can think now of a few men who do this consistently for me, and their friendship is one of the great treasures of my life.

8. When David was in trouble, Jonathan went to him and "strengthened his hand in God" (1 Samuel 23:16). In this way he encouraged David to take the risk of staying his course. Do you have someone who "strengthens your hand in God"? Someone who not only comforts and encourages, but urges you, through God, to cut loose from the moorings of living safely in the harbor and to move out into the risky but joyous waters of what Christ is calling you to? Are you that kind of person for someone else? Record your response to these questions here:

A Fresh Look at Ministry

The nineteenth-century English clergyman Frederic William Farrar pictured every believer's soul as "a cavern full of gems."

> The casual observer glances into it through some cranny, and all looks dark and sullen and useless. But let light enter into it and lo! It will flash with crystals and amethysts and quiver under the touch of brightness.
>
> If souls do not shine before you it is because you bring them no light to make them shine. Throw away your miserable, smouldering, fuming torch of conceit and hatred, lift up to them the light of love, and lo! They will arise and shine; yea, flame and burn with an undreamt of glory.

What does it mean to minister to others in such a way as to cause God's light to fall on their hidden gems, making them blaze forth for His glory?

"Our sufficiency is from God," Paul said, "who also made us sufficient as *ministers of the new covenant*" (2 Corinthians 3:5-6). What does it look like to minister to others from a New Covenant approach?

This same passage is where Paul said, "The letter kills, but the Spirit gives life" (3:6). Old Covenant ministry breeds death. A ministry that merely lays before people a code to live by—and reproves them for not being disciplined or committed enough to keep it—drains away vitality, joy, and hope.

But New Covenant ministry infuses life as it spotlights the excellence of Christ and the outlandish resources He has provided for us, as it calls us to the high adventure of living unreservedly for the King of kings.

Paul spoke also in this passage of the Old Covenant "ministry of condemnation" (3:9). Old Covenant ministry is shame-based and guilt-driven as it focuses primarily on where we fall short of God's standards.

But New Covenant ministry arouses hope—confident expectation and blazing optimism. While it doesn't back away at all from confronting sin and disobedience, it always moves beyond the failure to the possibility. It seeks to arouse the godly inclination in all believers to know God more deeply, to hunger for His best, and to move forward in His power to the only way of life that can genuinely satisfy their new hearts.

New Covenant ministry, like the New Covenant itself, is a radically new and better way to stimulate growth in believers' lives. It's working *with* God in helping other believers fulfill their whole potential in Christ.

What It Looks Like

9. Imagine chatting with a Christian friend who confides that he's feeling guilty for not praying more. He asks you for help and advice. What would you say to this friend? What would you say…

(a) if you were responding in an Old Covenant way?

(b) if you were responding in a New Covenant way?

If you answer the previous question from an Old Covenant approach, you might say something like this:

"You know, John, God specifically commands us to pray. In fact, He says to pray without ceasing. It seems to me that if praying were important enough to you, you could find the time. It doesn't matter whether you feel like it or not; what matters is whether you're going to obey Him. If you're going to be a committed believer, prayer is one of the most important disciplines you need to be doing."

On the other hand, a New Covenant approach might be this:

"When you became a believer, John, one of the many great things that happened to you is that God placed within you a desire to communicate with Him. This desire can never be taken away, because God made the promise to give His people a heart to know Him. I know that this desire may not seem real to you right now, but I can assure you it's still there.

"In fact, my guess is that even as we're talking, you're beginning to sense this desire stirring within you. Prayer is one of the primary ways we communicate with God, and for you to experience the kind of intimacy with Him that I know you want to have, you need to talk with Him. That's what prayer is really all about. And you know what? God Himself will give you strength and even wisdom for your praying.

"I know you want more out of your relationship with God than you're tasting now, and prayer offers you such a big part of experiencing God's best for your life."

New Covenant ministry is based upon positive, God-given assumptions about every believer. A New Covenant approach to ministry views all believers through *fundamentally optimistic lenses.* "From now on," Paul said, "we regard no one according to the flesh.... If anyone is in Christ, he is a new creation; old things have passed away; behold, all things have become new" (2 Corinthians 5:16-17). Or to put it another way, we no longer view believers primarily in light of their *problems* but in light of their *potential* because of the Holy Spirit dwelling within them.

Fellow brothers and sisters in Christ are not just forgiven sinners. They are silver saints who possess something wonderful beneath the tarnish of their sinful nature. For every believer there's something deeper in them than their sin, no matter how obscured it may be.

What You Can Know for Certain

What are these positive assumptions you can be certain of for every believer?

First, every Christian you encounter is of immense value and importance. Not only did Christ die for them, but God also has uniquely designed them to be an exhibition of the supernatural—a reflection of His craftsmanship. This is true for *every* believer; there are no disposable saints. We're all "His workmanship, created in Christ Jesus for good works, which God prepared beforehand that we should walk in them" (Ephesians 2:10). To help accomplish these divinely ordained good works, God has also given each believer one or more spiritual gifts for carrying out His will.

Therefore our calling is not to help other believers fulfill what *we* think is the will of God for their lives, but to help them hear the voice of God *for themselves* and find their unique, God-designed, God-gifted calling.

With every believer you encounter, we can also assume this person will never be fully satisfied until his or her life is fully aligned with God's uniquely designed purposes. No matter how content he may look on the outside, there'll be some measure of internal restlessness if this believer's life is out of alignment with God's purposes.

Sometimes I'll ask a Christian brother, "Do you feel like you're hitting on all six cylinders spiritually, in terms of the direction your life is headed?" Or, "If you were to die tomorrow, would you basically be satisfied with how you've spent the last few years of your life?" Very often the answer is "no," and then I can begin to help him explore the reasons.

We can also assume that every believer we encounter has divinely implanted resources that are pressing outward for release. Our calling is not to make something happen within him but simply to help release what God has already set in motion.

Jesus made this promise for every believer: "Out of his heart will flow rivers of living water" (John 7:38). The waters of the life of Christ relentlessly push forward for expression from within all of us. Some believers may not be aware of this, but they cannot thwart its reality. If the waters aren't making their way past the surface, it's not because they've stopped pressing, but because the believer has shut the floodgates of his life for one reason or another. Our responsibility is *not* to get the waters moving, but to cooperate with the Holy Spirit in helping open up those gates again.

THE MESSAGES YOU CONVEY

Christlike love is the lifeblood of our ministry, for Christ's New Covenant command is to love one another *as He loved us* (John 13:34). As we seek to love other believers in this way, what messages will our love convey?

The first is this: *I'm relentlessly and unconditionally for you. You can never extinguish my love for you.*

Our love is to be like the love of Christ, who loved His disciples "to the end" (John 13:1), even as they denied and deserted Him. It's a love that "bears all things, believes all things, hopes all things, endures all things," a love that "never fails" (1 Corinthians 13:7-8). This love communicates loudly and clearly, "You do not have to change in order to maintain my love for you."

At times it may need to be a tough love. It might even require, if absolutely necessary, breaking fellowship with the loved one, though this is always to be done out of love and never for lack of it. The key issue is that our ministry be bathed in a supernatural, relentless love for the ones God has privileged us to influence.

Another message our love should communicate is this: *I see your potential for the kingdom of God and it excites me. I'll do all I can to help see this purpose realized.*

New Covenant love is as purposeful as it is unconditional. I like to think of it this way. True love provides both a *home* and a *business*. It provides a home in the sense that the loved one enjoys the safe place of love's unfailing warmth. It provides a business in the sense that the loved one is encouraged to find and live out his calling, thereby fulfilling what he was made for.

A final message our love should send is this: *I'll do all I can to help inflame your new nature. I'll also stand against your flesh when necessary.*

Again, both aspects are critical. True love requires that we be wise physicians, knowing when to nourish the healthy tissue and when to do battle against the cancer.

God: Present or Absent?

New Covenant ministry is, above all else, working with God—not working *for* God, but *with* Him. The distinction between these two is literally the difference between the presence or absence of God in our ministry.

He hasn't delegated something as serious as *His* ministry into unaided hands like yours or mine. What He has set out for us to do, He fully intends to do *Himself.*

Yet He has chosen to do this through the unlikely medium of flesh and blood, you and me. As in Zechariah's day, our ministry from beginning to end is to be shot through with our Lord's key ingredient for success—" 'Not by might nor by power, but by My Spirit,' says the LORD of hosts" (Zechariah 4:6).

In summary, I would define New Covenant ministry as working with God to help others fulfill their whole potential in Christ (Colossians 1:28-29). This is done in large measure by (1) nourishing and stimulating the new nature, (2) exposing the perversity and foolishness of living by the flesh, and (3) beckoning to a more God-honoring and personally satisfying plane of living.

Conclusion: Time for a Revolution

My fervent hope is that what you've discovered in this workbook will lead you to more and more of the glorious adventure of supernatural living, causing you by God's grace to soar to new heights of Spirit-wrought godliness and impact.

This soaring will inevitably take us into the dark and turbulent winds of suffering, trials, and heartache. While this hasn't been an issue I've addressed throughout this workbook, it's a large and critical part of godly living. The Scriptures promise us undeserved suffering and admonish us to endure it as part of our calling. However, we're called not just to suffer, but to suffer *well*—in a God-honoring fashion that displays the supernatural in the midst of our trials. For this to happen absolutely requires the provisions of the New Covenant.

In closing, let me express my conviction that the time has come for a spiritual revolution founded upon New Covenant sanctification. I don't say this lightly or easily. This revolution will not occur overnight, nor will it go unopposed. But it is desperately needed. No one can look at the state of the church today and not agree that *something* is missing—badly missing in many cases. People are routinely either burned or bored by their experience with church; many never give Christianity a second look.

We owe it to God and to this dying world to give a clear glimpse of the true

---

A New Covenant Prayer

May the beauty of Christ be my focus...

the strength of Christ my dependency...

the approval of Christ my contentment...

the word of Christ my meditation...

the leading of Christ my agenda...

the presence of Christ my feast...

and the glory of Christ my mission.

Christ through our daily lives. For this to happen, the provisions of the New Covenant are not merely a good option; they are absolute essentials.

I see encouraging signs from many quarters that this revolution is beginning. It goes by different names but has one central message: Christ Himself is as much the key to sanctification as He is to justification. More and more thirsty hearts are tasting the new wine of New Covenant living, and as a result they will no longer settle for stale religiosity or dry rule keeping.

May God mightily increase their number for the sake of His glory. May you be counted among them.

10. (a) How would you summarize the most significant things you have learned from going through *Experiencing Christ Within?*

(b) What do you believe God wants most for you to do in your life as a result of going through this workbook?

(c) How would you talk this over with God? Write your response here as a prayer to Him.

OPTIONAL FURTHER STUDY (FOR GOING IN-DEPTH)

Intimacy with God

1. Read 1 Corinthians 2:9-12. What does this passage teach us about the role of the Spirit in experiencing God firsthand?

2. Reflect on John 4:14. According to this passage, what is the role of the Spirit within every believer?

Freedom in Christ

3. Meditate on Galatians 5:1. What do you think Paul means here by "freedom" or "liberty"? And what does he mean by the "yoke of bondage" or "of slavery"?

4. *Reflect on John 8:31-36. What do you think Jesus fully meant by the phrase "free indeed"?*

Community

5. *How would you state in your own words the New Covenant promise that God makes in Jeremiah 32:39?*

6. *Meditate on Ephesians 4:1-6. Express in your own words how this passage reflects what God's Spirit does for us as believers.*

Ministry

7. *Reflect on 2 Corinthians 2:14–3:6. What are the key elements of New Covenant ministry as you find them in these verses?*

Guidelines for the Group Discussion Leader

Our Calling to Supernatural Living

Week One: A Brand-New Arrangement

You may want to review or even read aloud some of the content in "A Quick Introduction: Ready for Release"—especially the material under the headings "So What's New?" and "Where Is the Gospel's Power?" and "Not Fixing, But Releasing."

You may also want to spend time reviewing the group's various answers to question 1 in this week's lesson—about their personal goals and expectations for this course.

It might also be good to spend time discussing the group's answers for questions 6, 9, 12, and 13 in this lesson on pages 15-28.

A. How would you describe or define the fundamental differences between the Old and New Covenants? And why is it important in our everyday Christian lives to know these differences?

B. According to your best understanding, in what significant ways is the New Covenant radically *superior* to the Old Covenant?

C. Under the heading "Make a Clean Break," the content begins with these questions: "But what's really so wrong about mixing a little Old Covenant into our lives? Won't it cause people to live more fully for God?" Do you completely agree with the way these questions are answered in the lesson? In what ways, if any, are you unconvinced?

D. Where in your life have you found that God's law agitates your flesh? Give a specific example.

E. Under the heading "Into His Arms" we find this statement: "The Old Covenant provided a code to live under; the New Covenant provides *a Person to live through.*" What does this mean? (Think of as many ramifications as you can.) And to what degree is this a new thought for you?

F. Under the heading "The Desire Is There," what was your reaction to this statement: "Within every believer, the desire to do the will of God is the gift of God"? Are you fully convinced this is true? If not, what questions do you have about this?

G. Has this chapter influenced how you view the kind of obedience God desires? If so, in what way? Is this kind of obedience appealing to you? Or does it seem even more burdensome than ever?

H. What did you find most helpful in this week's lesson? What did you find troubling or confusing?

THE HIGHER PURPOSE OF SUPERNATURAL LIVING

Week Two: FIRST THINGS FIRST: A REPUTATION AT STAKE

For fruitful discussion, some of the best questions in the lesson for discussing the group's answers include questions 2, 7, and 12.

A. This lesson stated that what matters most to God is *not* people. How did you react to that statement? (See your answers to question 11.) Is this a new thought for you?

B. In a way that's most meaningful for you, how would you define or describe God's *glory?* God's *name?*

C. If God commands us to be humble and unconcerned for our reputation— why does *He* seem to do the exact opposite of this? Do you find this issue unsettling? What helps you resolve it?

D. What was God's primary purpose for Israel, and how, specifically, were His people to accomplish this? And why is it helpful for us to know this?

E. What is God's primary purpose for the church? How are we to accomplish this? Again, be specific.

F. Have you seen another believer genuinely glorify God in a real and concrete way? How did he or she do this?

G. What are some of the ways you see the name of God being "profaned" by Christians today?

H. Have your perspectives or attitudes changed in any significant way as a result of this week's lesson? If so, talk about this.

I. What struggles do you still have with any of the major points taught in this week's lesson?

Week Three: BECOMING SPIRITUALLY PROVOCATIVE

You may want to spend time discussing the group's answers for questions 11 and 13 in this lesson.

A. Think again about the following statement (found on this lesson's opening page): "God's goal for our lives [is] to make us not just spiritually *whole* but spiritually *provocative*." What's the real difference between these two?

B. Recall the content in the section entitled "Unique Applications," which focuses on various answers John gave to different groups of people in Luke 3 when they asked him, "What shall we do?" Identify some of the leading groups in your own community (especially occupational categories—businesspeople, homemakers, government workers, military, students, etc.). If John were transported across time to today, how might he answer that question for each of the groups you identified?

C. You may want to especially review and discuss the group's answers to questions 4-8 in this week's lesson, about how glorifying God can make a difference in various aspects of our lives.

D. The section entitled "Ingodded People" speaks of the great value of "being supremely preoccupied with God's greatness and presence." How does such a preoccupation fit into having what we might call a "balanced" life, one in which we meet all our responsibilities and obligations? Is preoccupation with God actually possible, without getting our lives "out of balance"? Explain your answer.

E. Think again about the John Piper quote in this section, where he says, "God's deepest commitment to be glorified and my deepest longing to be satisfied are not in conflict, but in fact find simultaneous consummation" when we glorify God. In everyday terms, how would you explain what he means by that? Is this a new thought for you? Is it helpful?

F. In what aspect of your life or thinking has this week's lesson made the most difference?

Our Desperate Need for Supernatural Living

Week Four: The Journey to Radical Dependence

You may want to discuss the group's answers for questions 1, 10, 12, and 15 in this lesson.

A. How would you describe the various directions our flesh gravitates toward? Which kind of "rat" does your own flesh lean toward—scraggly and smelly, or well groomed and respectable? Or something else?

B. Under the sidebar entitled "Swim and Sink—or Be Saved" we find this statement: "The end of ourselves is the beginning of God." What does it actually mean to come to the "end" of ourselves? Is this a one-time event, or a recurring process?

C. Under the heading "Mud in a Slum" we read that "God has created us with deep cravings in our spirit especially for *relationship* and for *impact*." How have you seen this as being true in your own life? Which of the two—relationship or impact—do you personally long for most?

D. From the same section of this week's lesson, ponder this statement: "Ultimately all sin is taking one of these God-given longings and going in a God-absent direction to fulfill it." Can you think of some examples of this? Why is it ineffective to simply tell people to stay away from the wrong things, or say no to them? Or is it ineffective?

E. How do you respond to the C. S. Lewis quote under the heading "Sins of the Flesh, Sins of the Spirit"? What are some examples of each kind of sin? Which kind would you say is actually worse, and why? Or are they equally bad?

F. Under the heading "What, Why, How," review the three elements mentioned there that must be present for God to consider a work truly "good" in His sight. Which of these three standards do you generally find the most difficult to attain?

G. What words would you use to describe our moral and spiritual capabilities apart from God's indwelling power? Can you give an example of how you've seen the limits of these capabilities in your own life?

H. Under the heading "God's Good Intent, and His Good Remedy," this lesson states that "God's intent in clearly exposing our sinfulness is not to make us feel bad. It's to make us feel desperate." In everyday terms, what does it actually mean to feel "desperate" in this way? How is that different from only feeling bad? Is it possible to have true repentance without such desperation?

I. What kinds of subtle reliance on the flesh are easiest for you?

GOD'S PROVISIONS FOR OUR SUPERNATURAL LIVING

Week Five: RELEASING YOUR NEW PURITY

You may want to invite the group's discussion of their answers to questions 4, 5, and 12 in this lesson.

A. Look again at the opening quotation from A. W. Tozer under the lesson title. How would you explain what Tozer meant by these words? Why must we take refuge *from* God?

B. In what ways, if any, has your view of God been affected by this week's lesson?

C. Think about this phrase (from the section entitled "Off the Chart"): "Assumed grace can never be transforming grace." In what ways do you feel the church today might be merely assuming the grace of God?

D. Under the heading "Our Alien Clothing" we find Luther's term "alien righteousness" to describe the righteousness God places upon us as believers. In what various ways is it "alien" to us? Think of as many as you can.

E. How would you describe the difference between forgiveness, cleansing, and being clothed in Christ's righteousness? Which of these three is the hardest for you to fully believe and appreciate?

F. Is it true that all our relationships with other people are motivated either *from* acceptance or *for* acceptance? How does our new purity ensure that we can always relate to others *from* acceptance?

G. Is it difficult for you to visualize God smiling from ear to ear as He looks down on you? What other expression do you most often expect on His face when He looks at you? (See your answers to questions 13 and 15.)

H. In the same section, look at your answers to question 14. Could you identify with any parts of the struggling missionary's testimony?

I. Do you believe God has been speaking to you through this week's lesson? If so, what is the most important thing He's taught you?

Week Six: Dangerous—and Worth the Risk

Some good questions in this lesson for exploring the group's answers include questions 1, 6, 7, 9, 12, and 13.

A. What have you learned about God's grace in this week's lesson? Do you see it in a different way now? If so, how?

B. What are some specific ways the church tries to "safeguard" grace?

C. How have you experienced grace from another person in a deeply memorable way?

D. What has helped you most to see God's grace as something experiential more than doctrinal? Or is it still hard to view it that way?

E. Think again about the parable of the prodigal son in Luke 15. In the way Jesus told this story, what actions by the father are most meaningful to you? Why?

F. This lesson speaks of a "vigorous" assurance of salvation as opposed to a "tentative" one. What other terms can you think of to describe the kind of salvation assurance that you're convinced God wants us to have? In what ways have you seen the church offer only "tentative" assurances of salvation?

G. Why is the doctrine of eternal security so important to our proper understanding and experience of God's grace?

H. Under the heading "Putting Our New Purity to Work," Romans 4:5 is described as "one of the clearest verses in the Bible that describe true saving faith." How do you see this verse demonstrating (a) a recognition of personal need, (b) the refusal to trust in any personal effort or religious rite, and (c) a sole reliance on the justification that comes from God through Christ?

I. In this lesson (under the heading "Secure Enough to Love") we find the statement "Only secure people can love well." Do you agree or disagree with that assertion? And why?

J. How would you summarize what God does to give us security in our relationships with others?

K. What for you was the most meaningful concept or truth in this week's lesson?

Week Seven: RELEASING YOUR NEW IDENTITY

Good questions in this lesson for exploring the group's answers include 1, 10, 11, 12, and 13.

A. How would you describe what really happened to you at conversion? Did anything in this lesson help deepen your understanding of what it means to be a "new creation" in Christ? If so, what?

B. Recall the Jonathan Edwards statement (under the heading "What No Pill Can Do") that Christ has become for us "*inherent* as well as *imputed* righteousness." What's the difference between the two? How would you describe in your own words the change that our conversion has accomplished in both our *position* and our *condition?*

C. In regard to sin, have you tended in the past to view yourself as more like costume jewelry or like tarnished silver? How do you view yourself now?

D. Is a godly self-image important? If so, why? What difference does it actually make?

E. In what ways does the world offer to improve our personal identity? Why is God's way so much better?

F. Notice again the statement (under the heading "Getting Used to Justification") that "sanctification is simply the art of getting used to justification." What does that mean, in practical terms? Is this a new thought to you?

G. What things seem most often to get in the way of believing and appropriating our new identity?

H. What parts of this week's lesson did you find most helpful? What parts did you find confusing or disturbing?

Week Eight: YOUR NEWNESS GOES PUBLIC

You may want to discuss the group's answers for questions 5 and 6 in this week's lesson.

A. From what you've studied in this lesson, has your understanding of sanctification changed? If so, in what way?

B. This lesson says (under the heading "God's Very Nature Within"), "A good self-image is not *developed* but rather *received.*" What does this mean in everyday terms? What are some ways we try to develop our self-image rather than humbly receive it?

C. In what wrong places are you most tempted to look for your identity?

D. Under the heading "More Wrong Labels," this lesson says, "No Christian has a damaged soul. What we all have is wrinkled flesh." Why is it important to make this distinction? What difference does it make?

E. During the past week, in what ways have you sensed your own inadequacy? What might have been the source of your identity at that moment?

F. How will a full understanding of our new identity affect the way we view sin? Sanctification? Righteousness? Christian service? God's glory?

G. How can we practically remind ourselves that sin is not only wrong, but also foolish? In what ways is it foolish? (See your answers to Question 9.) Can you think of Scripture passages that demonstrate this?

H. In the past week, what's the most meaningful thing God has inwardly spoken to you through His Spirit and His Word?

Week Nine: RELEASING YOUR NEW DISPOSITION

You may want to invite the group's discussion of their answers to questions 3, 7, 8, and 13 in this lesson.

A. Look again at the contrasts given in the sidebar entitled "Obedience False and True." What thoughts here impacted you most? Was there anything you disagreed with? How would you describe in your own words the difference between serving "in the newness of the Spirit" versus "the oldness of the letter" (Romans 7:6)?

B. Review the group's answers to part (b) in question 1. How are we to unleash and experience both our God-given power and our God-given desire to obey and please Him?

C. In this lesson, what new perspectives, if any, did you come across regarding our natural heart (the flesh) and its attitude toward God and spirituality? Were you surprised or even offended at anything you read here?

D. Notice the three numbered points in the "No Longer Shocked" sidebar. In what specific ways could these reminders be helpful for you when you encounter sinful thoughts?

E. In what specific ways have you learned to rely on God's implanted *desire* for obeying and pleasing Him?

F. Under the heading "What Our New Heart Is Like" are the statements that we can neither love God nor fear God "unaided." Are these statements an encouragement for you? Or do you think they minimize our legitimate responsibility in loving and fearing God?

G. Has God deeply impressed something upon you through this week's lesson? If so, discuss its significance for you.

Week Ten: BOTH FAITH AND FEELINGS

Good questions in this lesson for exploring the group's answers include 1, 2, 5, 6, and 7.

A. How did you respond to the statement (under the heading "What About Emotions?") that "it's impossible not to live by feelings"? Can you think of any verses to support this assertion?

B. Is there any significant danger in living either too much or too little by emotions? If so, what's the actual danger in each case?

C. Under the heading "Duty or Desire?" we're reminded of the biblical truth that we're to "serve the LORD with gladness"—as well as the fact that this gladness "ultimately can come only from God Himself through His gift of our new disposition." How can we fully rely on and tap into that gift in order to obey God's standard for glad-heartedness as we serve Him?

D. When would it be right to ask God to change our hearts? When would it be wrong? What scripture do you know that supports your answers? In what ways are you convinced that God has already changed your heart? Can you think of any cases where you've asked God for spiritual things that He actually has already given you?

E.   Why is becoming a radically abandoned disciple of Christ "the greatest favor a believer can do himself"? What happens in our lives when we resist this abandonment?

F.   Ponder well the statement (under the heading "Unrestrained Indulgence") that "true obedience is the unrestrained indulgence of our new nature." Does this represent a new way of thinking for you? What does this indulgence mean to you in practical terms?

G.   In what ways, if any, do you find it helpful to think of spiritual disciplines as "spiritual connectors for spiritual indulgence"? How could this way of thinking be helpful in overcoming struggles you may have with any particular spiritual discipline?

H.   In what aspect of your life or thinking has this week's lesson made the most difference?

Week Eleven: RELEASING YOUR NEW POWER

You may want to invite discussion of the group's answers for questions 13, 17, 19, 20, and 21 in this lesson.

A.   On the first page of this week's lesson, look again at the "equation" shown there that leads to frustration and defeat. Do you agree with what this equation is saying? In what ways, if any, have you seen this to be true in your own life?

B.   Why do you think God has made us so dependent on His power? How does this fit with the importance He places on His own glory? How does this fit with His love for us?

C.   "Whenever the "should's" of the Christian life become our central focus, we revert to living under a code (the letter) rather than through a Person (the Spirit)." Think again about that statement from the section entitled "Skis,

But No Boat." Where in your own life have you sensed a wrong focus on the "should's"? What kinds of "should's" are most likely to keep us from focusing upon Christ through the Holy Spirit?

D. Under the heading "Wanting a Piece of the Action," we read the assertion that "our problem isn't in *trusting* God; it's in trusting God *alone*." Do you think that statement is entirely true? What most likely is the root of our not being willing to trust God alone?

E. Take some time to review your study of Romans 7:14-25 as reflected in questions 9-11. Were there any portions of that passage that you found unclear? What parts of the passage did you find most encouraging and helpful?

F. What does it mean in practical, everyday terms to truly embrace your inadequacy (as opposed to just "admitting" it)? What can keep us from fully doing this?

G. Think again about these bold words (under the heading "Empowerment for Impact"): "*God will never call you to something you can do.* Period. If you can do what God has called you to *without* the new power God alone provides...*then you missed what God has called you to.* God calls us only to that which requires Him." How fully do you agree with these statements? In what ways, if any, do you disagree? Have you seen the truth of these words in your own life? If so, how?

H. In what particular ways, if any, was this lesson especially helpful for you?

Week Twelve: DYNAMIC DEPENDENCE

For fruitful discussion, you may want to discuss the group's answers for questions 7 and 8 in this lesson.

A. Take some time to review your study of John 15:1-8 as reflected in each part of question 2. In your own words and in a way that's most practically helpful for you, how would you describe what it means to "abide" (or "remain") in Christ, as this passage speaks of it? (See your answer to part c of question 2.

B. Can you think of a time in your life when you experienced a degree of dependence on God that was significantly deeper than normal? If so, describe what this was like. What was your level of joy at that time? And how close did you feel to Him?

C. What kinds of things typically keep us from relying on the Father with the same consistency of dependence that Jesus demonstrated? Where do you struggle most with this?

D. How would you describe the difference between "spiritual" leadership (in true reliance on God) and merely "natural" leadership?

E. Review the content under the sidebar heading "Upward, Inward, Outward." What do these passages mean practically to you? How do they help you most in understanding the Holy Spirit's ministry?

F. Take a moment to look together at Galatians 5:16-25, and notice the different words and phrases used there to describe our dependence on the Holy Spirit and His guidance and control in our lives. How would you summarize the essence of what those terms mean?

G. What are the most significant ways God has spoken to you this week through your study?

THE PRACTICAL OUTWORKING OF SUPERNATURAL LIVING

Week Thirteen: THE ADVENTURE CONTINUES

Because of the length of this lesson, you may want to plan to cover it in two weeks instead of one.

Some of the best questions in the lesson for discussing the group's answers include questions 2, 3, 4, 5, 6, and 10.

A. How do you respond to the term "Christian mysticism" as it's referred to in this lesson? Do you agree with Francis Schaeffer's description of it? In what ways, if any, do you think Christians should more fully apply this concept of mysticism? What Scripture passages do you know that can help us better understand this?

B. In practical terms, what significant differences do you think it could make in your sense of intimacy with God to have a rich and full understanding of the New Covenant truths taught in this workbook?

C. How would you define or describe true freedom in Christ? Where do you feel the greatest need for this freedom in your own life?

D. In practical terms, what significant differences do you think it could make in the degree of freedom in Christ you experience to have a rich and full understanding of the New Covenant truths taught in this workbook?

E. Under the heading "A Fresh Look at Community" we find the Dietrich Bonhoeffer statement that "Christian brotherhood is not an ideal which we must realize; it is rather a reality created by God in Christ in which we may participate." How do you respond to this statement? Is this statement in itself too ideal and abstract? Or do you see rich truth here that can make a genuine and significant difference in how we relate to other believers?

F. In practical terms, what significant differences do you think it could make in your relationships with other Christians—in worship, service, and fellowship—to have a rich and full understanding of the New Covenant truths taught in this workbook?

G. How would you describe in your own words the fundamental differences between a New Covenant approach to ministry and an Old Covenant approach? And what is the actual impact of those differences for the people involved in each?

H. In practical terms, what significant differences do you think it could make in your own ministry to others to have a rich and full understanding of the New Covenant truths taught in this workbook?

Notes

A Quick Introduction: READY FOR RELEASE

page

006   "The whole dispensation of the Spirit": Andrew Murray, *The Two Covenants* (1898; reprint, Fort Washington, Pa.: Christian Literature Crusade, 1974), 5-6.

008   "substantial healing": Francis A. Schaeffer, *True Spirituality* (Wheaton, Ill.: Tyndale, 1971), 134.

008   "To the great loss of the church": J. Oswald Sanders, *Spiritual Lessons* (Chicago: Moody, 1944), 89.

Week One: A BRAND-NEW ARRANGEMENT

page

011   "Discipleship is built": Oswald Chambers, *My Utmost for His Highest: An Updated Edition in Today's Language,* ed. James Reimann (1935; reprint, Grand Rapids, Mich.: Discovery House, 1992), October 21 reading.

020   "All these names": Andrew Murray, *The Two Covenants* (1898; reprint, Fort Washington, Pa.: Christian Literature Crusade, 1974), 51.

021   "favored…in preaching Christ crucified": David Brainerd, as quoted in Jonathan Edwards, "Life and Diary of the Rev. David Brainerd," *The Works of Jonathan Edwards*, vol. 2 (Edinburgh: The Banner of Truth and Trust, 1834), 416-7.

021 "The law demands": Blaise Pascal, *Pensées,* Everyman edition (New York: Dutton, 1958), pensée #521, 142.

022 "We receive an inward fervency": Martin Luther, *Commentary on Galatians,* ed. John Prince Fallows, trans. Erasmus Middleton (Grand Rapids, Mich.: Kregel, 1979), 238.

025 approaches to spiritual maturity: Larry Crabb, *Connecting* (Nashville: Word, 1997), 39.

027 Charles Spurgeon's story of poor woman: *All of Grace* (Springdale, Pa.: Whitaker House, 1981), 7.

Week Two: FIRST THINGS FIRST: A REPUTATION AT STAKE

page

031 "Put first things first": C. S. Lewis, *Letters of C. S. Lewis,* ed. Walter Hooper and W. H. Lewis (New York: Harcourt, Brace, 1966), 228; letter of 23 April 1951, par. 2.

033 "on the side of the North": Abraham Lincoln, as quoted in Rev. Matthew Simpson, *Funeral Address Delivered at the Burial of President Lincoln* (New York: Carlton & Porter, 1865), 16.

034 "Utilitarian Christ": A. W. Tozer, *The Root of the Righteous* (Harrisburg, Pa.: Christian Publications, 1955), 23.

039 "first duty": John Calvin, as quoted in Charles W. Colson, *Loving God* (Grand Rapids, Mich.: Zondervan, 1983), 176.

040 Henry Stanley on David Livingstone, as quoted in Ruth A. Tucker, *From Jerusalem to Irian Jaya* (Grand Rapids, Mich.: Zondervan, 1983), 153.

042 "should also be beautiful": Francis Schaeffer, *True Spirituality* (Wheaton, Ill.: Tyndale, 1971), 177.

043 "best argument": Sheldon Vanauken, *A Severe Mercy* (San Francisco: Harper & Row, 1977), 85.

046   "Put first things first": Lewis, *Letters of C. S. Lewis.*

Week Three: BECOMING SPIRITUALLY PROVOCATIVE

page

054   "Every disability": C. S. Lewis in a letter to Sheldon Vanauken, as quoted in Sheldon Vanauken, *A Severe Mercy* (San Francisco: Harper & Row, 1977), 147.

055   "how to use God": Eugene Nida, as related to me by Walt Baker, missions professor at Dallas Theological Seminary, from a personal conversation with Dr. Eugene Nida.

056   "true way to be humble": Phillips Brooks, source unknown.

059   "simultaneous consummation": John Piper, *The Supremacy of God in Preaching* (Grand Rapids, Mich.: Baker, 1990), 26.

Week Four: THE JOURNEY TO RADICAL DEPENDENCE

page

068   "mud pies": C. S. Lewis, "The Weight of Glory," in *The Weight of Glory and Other Addresses* (1949; reprint, New York: Macmillan, 1980), 4.

068   "Through the whole of the Old Covenant": Andrew Murray, *The Two Covenants* (1898; reprint, Fort Washington, Pa.: Christian Literature Crusade, 1974), 28.

071   "sins of the flesh": C. S. Lewis, *Mere Christianity* (New York: Macmillan, 1960), 94-5.

073   "drunken peasant": Martin Luther, as quoted in *What Luther Says,* comp. Ewald M. Plass (St. Louis: Concordia, 1959), 1533.

074   "by direct moral effort": C. S. Lewis, *Mere Christianity,* 165.

078   "so many recesses": John Calvin, *Institutes,* trans. Henry Beveridge (Grand Rapids, Mich.: Eerdmans, 1962), 478.

079   "When the law constrains a man": Martin Luther, *Commentary on Galatians,* ed. John Prince Fallows, trans. Erasmus Middleton (Grand Rapids, Mich.: Kregel, 1979), 205.

Week Five: RELEASING YOUR NEW PURITY

page

082   "from God in God": A. W. Tozer, *The Knowledge of the Holy* (San Francisco: Harper & Row, 1961), 114.

082   George Wilson story: *United States v Wilson,* 32 U.S. 150, 7 Pet. 150, 8 L.Ed. 640 (U.S.Pa. 1833).

085   "grandfather in Heaven": C. S. Lewis, *The Problem of Pain* (New York: Macmillan, 1962), 28.

086   "God of White-Hot Rage": John White, *The Race* (Downers Grove, Ill.: InterVarsity, 1984), 25, 33.

086   "God dwells in light": Martin Luther, as quoted in Roland Bainton, *Here I Stand* (Nashville: Abingdon, 1950), 43.

087   "God to manageable terms": Tozer, *The Knowledge of the Holy,* 10.

088   "How wonderful, how beautiful": F. W. Faber, as quoted in J. Oswald Sanders, *Prayer Power Unlimited* (Chicago: Moody Press, 1977), 20.

089   R. C. Sproul on Jonathan Edwards's sermon: R. C. Sproul, *The Holiness of God* (Wheaton, Ill.: Tyndale, 1988), 224.

090   "It would be dreadful": Jonathan Edwards, "Sinners in the Hands of an Angry God," *The Works of Jonathan Edwards,* vol. 2 (Edinburgh: The Banner of Truth and Trust, 1834), 11.

092   "eucatastrophe": J. R. R. Tolkien, "On Fairy-Stories," *Tree and Leaf* (1964; reprint, New York: Houghton Mifflin, 1989), 62.

098   "Jesus paid it all": lyrics by Elvina M. Hall.

Week Six: DANGEROUS—AND WORTH THE RISK

page

104   "Then suddenly there dawns": Paul Tournier, *Guilt and Grace,* trans. Arthur W. Heathcote (San Francisco: Harper & Row, 1983), 193.

113   "no better test": D. Martyn Lloyd-Jones, *Romans: An Exposition of Chapter 6* (Grand Rapids, Mich.: Zondervan, 1972), 8.

116   "the 'yes' of the heart": Martin Luther, as quoted in *What Luther Says,* comp. Ewald M. Plass (St. Louis: Concordia, 1959), 1376.

118   "Faith holds out the hand": Martin Luther, as quoted in Zane Hodges, *Absolutely Free* (Grand Rapids, Mich.: Zondervan, 1989), 227.

119   "Faith consists": J. Gresham Machen, *What Is Faith?* (Edinburgh: The Banner of Truth and Trust, 1925), 178.

120   "bedrock of our Christian faith": Oswald Chambers, *My Utmost for His Highest: An Updated Edition in Today's Language,* ed. James Reimann (1935; reprint, Grand Rapids, Mich.: Discovery House, 1992), March 7 reading.

Week Seven: RELEASING YOUR NEW IDENTITY

page

128   "inherent as well as imputed": Jonathan Edwards, "God Glorified in the Work of Redemption," *Jonathan Edwards: Basic Writings,* ed. Ola Elizabeth Winslow (New York: Penguin, 1966), 107.

128   costume jewelry or tarnished silver: I first heard this illustration from Robert Oliver, a good friend and pastor of Bastrop Bible Church.

133   "so entirely joined unto Christ": Martin Luther, *Commentary on Galatians,* ed. John Prince Fallows, trans. Erasmus Middleton (Grand Rapids, Mich.: Kregel, 1979), 90.

134 "actual deliverance": Edwards, "God Glorified in the Work of Redemption," 107.

136 "born crucified": L. E. Maxwell, *Born Crucified* (Chicago: Moody, 1945), 7.

136 "Sin need have no more power": Ruth Paxson, as quoted in Miles J. Stanford, *The Complete Green Letters* (Grand Rapids, Mich.: Zondervan, 1975), 50.

Week Eight: YOUR NEWNESS GOES PUBLIC

page

144 "God became man": C. S. Lewis, *Mere Christianity* (New York: Macmillan, 1960), 182.

150 "Should anyone knock": Martin Luther, as quoted in J. Oswald Sanders, *Paul the Leader* (Colorado Springs: NavPress, 1984), 74.

154 "suicidal abandonment of joy": John Piper, *God's Passion for His Glory* (Wheaton, Ill.: Crossway, 1998), 81.

154 "the rabbit in us": C. S. Lewis, *God in the Dock* (Grand Rapids, Mich.: Eerdmans, 1989), 112.

156 "angel trapped inside": Michelangelo, as quoted in *Sunday Sermons Treasury of Illustrations,* comp. James F. Colaianni (Pleasantville, N.J.: Voicings, 1982), 532.

Week Nine: RELEASING YOUR NEW DISPOSITION

page

158 "When the law is written": Andrew Murray, *The Two Covenants* (1898; reprint, Fort Washington, Pa.: Christian Literature Crusade, 1974), 117-8.

159 "holy, heavenly disposition": Jonathan Edwards, as quoted in *Closer Walk New Testament,* ed. Dr. Bruce H. Wilkinson (Grand Rapids, Mich.: Zondervan, 1990), 498.

161   "inbred distaste and disrelish": Jonathan Edwards, "Men Naturally Are God's Enemies," *The Works of Jonathan Edwards,* vol. 2 (Edinburgh: The Banner of Truth and Trust, 1834), 131.

163   "new, divine, and supernatural principles": Jonathan Edwards, "A Treatise Concerning Religious Affections," *The Works of Jonathan Edwards,* vol. 1 (Edinburgh: The Banner of Truth and Trust, 1834), 266-7.

164   "Grace not only saves the soul": C. H. Mackintosh, *Genesis to Deuteronomy* (1881; reprint, Neptune, N.J.: Loizeaux Brothers, 1972), 193.

167   "Human nature, if it is healthy": Oswald Chambers, as quoted in *Refresh, Renew, Revive,* ed. H. B. London Jr. (Colorado Springs: Focus on the Family, 1996), 73-4.

173   "moral consciousness…inherent": Renald Showers, *The New Nature* (Neptune, N.J.: Loizeaux Brothers, 1986), 48.

174   "The moment we believe": J. Oswald Sanders, *Spiritual Lessons,* rev. ed. (Chicago: Moody, 1971), 105.

Week Ten: BOTH FAITH AND FEELINGS

page

178   "The sense I had of divine things": Jonathan Edwards, "Personal Narrative," *Jonathan Edwards: Basic Writings,* ed. Ola Elizabeth Winslow (New York: Penguin, 1966), 84.

179   "in great part" of true "holy affections," "always a dynamic thing": Jonathan Edwards, "A Treatise Concerning Religious Affections," *The Works of Jonathan Edwards,* vol. 1 (Edinburgh: The Banner of Truth and Trust, 1834), 236.

179   "The first effect of the power of God": Jonathan Edwards, *Treatise on Grace,* ed. Paul Helm (Cambridge: James Clarke and Co., 1971), 48-9.

180   "They have spiritual excellency": Jonathan Edwards, "God Glorified in the Work of Redemption," *Jonathan Edwards: Basic Writings,* 115.

181   "God's aim is not to constrain men's submission": John Piper, *The Supremacy of God in Preaching* (Grand Rapids, Mich.: Baker, 1990), 25.

186   "get ahold of God": Oswald Chambers, *My Utmost for His Highest: An Updated Edition in Today's Language,* ed. James Reimann (1935; reprint, Grand Rapids, Mich.: Discovery House, 1992), February 7 reading.

186   "makes God real": R. A. Torrey, *How to Pray* (New Kensington, Pa.: Whitaker, 1983), 13.

186   "True prayer": Samuel Zwemer, *Into All the World* (Grand Rapids, Mich.: Zondervan, 1943), 160.

186   "perfect, overflowing, unutterable happiness": Charles Spurgeon, as quoted in J. O. Sanders, *The Divine Art of Soul-Winning* (n.p., 1937).

Week Eleven: RELEASING YOUR NEW POWER

page

189   "New Testament Christianity": D. Martyn Lloyd-Jones, *The Best of Martyn Lloyd-Jones,* comp. Christopher Catherwood (Grand Rapids, Mich.: Baker, 1993), 38.

190   "The ministry of the New Covenant": Andrew Murray, *The Two Covenants* (1898; reprint, Fort Washington, Pa.: Christian Literature Crusade, 1974), 141.

191   Thomas Carlyle story: *Illustrations for Preaching,* comp. Benjamin P. Browne (Nashville: Broadman, 1977), 54-5.

198   "Brokenness is the admission": Larry Crabb, "New Way Living," message given at Grace Bible Church, College Station, Texas, 8 April 2001.

201   "No good work is done anywhere": C. S. Lewis, *Reflections on the Psalms* (New York: Harcourt Brace Jovanovich, 1958), 110.

203   "Men are dependent on the power of God": Jonathan Edwards, "God Glorified in the Work of Redemption," *Jonathan Edwards: Basic Writings,* ed. Ola Elizabeth Winslow (New York: Penguin, 1966), 112.

Week Twelve: DYNAMIC DEPENDENCE

page

205   "The Spirit is an imperative necessity": A. W. Tozer, *Man: The Dwelling Place of God* (Harrisburg, Pa.: Christian Publications, 1966), 66.

206   "The redeemed are in every thing directly": Jonathan Edwards, "God Glorified in the Work of Redemption," *Jonathan Edwards: Basic Writings,* ed. Ola Elizabeth Winslow (New York: Penguin, 1966), 108.

214   "The spiritual leader": J. Oswald Sanders, *The Spiritual Leader* (Chicago: Moody, 1967), 33.

216   "active passivity": Francis Schaeffer, *The Complete Works of Francis A. Schaeffer: A Christian Worldview,* vol. 3, *A Christian View of Spirituality* (Wheaton, Ill.: Crossway, 1982), 281.

Week Thirteen: THE ADVENTURE CONTINUES

page

220   "God's deepest purpose": John Piper, *The Supremacy of God in Preaching* (Grand Rapids, Mich.: Baker, 1990), 24.

222   "He meant us to see Him": A. W. Tozer, *The Pursuit of God* (Camp Hill, Pa.: Christian Publications, 1982), 34.

223   "We pursue God because": Tozer, *The Pursuit of God,* 11.

225   "Christian mysticism": Francis Schaeffer, *True Spirituality* (Wheaton, Ill.: Tyndale, 1971), 54-5, 69-70.

227   "means different things to different people": Eugene Peterson, *Traveling Light* (Colorado Springs: Helmers & Howard, 1988), 57-8.

227   "A Christian is a perfectly free": Martin Luther, "The Freedom of a Christian," *Three Treatises* (Philadelphia: Fortress, 1943), 277.

229   "You may be able to compel people": Reinhold Niebuhr, as quoted in Charles R. Swindoll, *The Grace Awakening* (Nashville: Word, 1990), xv.

230   "prisms refracting the light": John Piper, *Desiring God* (Portland, Oreg.: Multnomah, 1986), 43.

232   disconnected from ourselves and others: Francis Schaeffer, *The Complete Works of Francis A. Schaeffer: A Christian Worldview*, vol. 3, *A Christian View of Spirituality* (Wheaton, Ill.: Crossway, 1982), 373-4.

232   "perfectly free lord of all": Luther, "The Freedom of a Christian," *Three Treatises,* 277.

233   "Christian brotherhood": Dietrich Bonhoeffer, *Life Together* (San Francisco: Harper & Row, 1954), 30.

235   "final apologetic": Francis Schaeffer, *The Church at the End of the Twentieth Century* (Downers Grove, Ill.: InterVarsity, 1970), 138.

237   "cavern full of gems": Frederic William Farrar, source unknown.

Acknowledgments

This workbook would never have been possible without the sacrifice, support, and encouragement of my wonderful family—my wife, Sandy, and our three fine sons, Stephen, Jordan, and Brandon. What a blessed man I am!

I also would like to express my deep gratitude to the elders, staff, and saints of Grace Bible Church in College Station, Texas. You have so richly blessed us over these past twenty years. How privileged I am to help pastor such choice servants of God.

Above all else, I want to thank Jesus Christ, who has brought me out of the miry clay, set my feet upon the Rock, and put a new song in my mouth. This book is in large measure that song.